# Voyages from the Past

*To dear Mum who loved people,*
*and always made them welcome.*

# Voyages from the Past

## A History of Passengers at Sea

Simon Wills

PEN & SWORD HISTORY

First published in Great Britain in 2014 by
Pen & Sword History
an imprint of
Pen & Sword Books Ltd
47 Church Street
Barnsley
South Yorkshire
S70 2AS

Copyright © Simon Wills 2014

ISBN 978 1 78303 636 3

Typeset in Ehrhardt by
Mac Style Ltd, Bridlington, East Yorkshire
Printed and bound in the UK by CPI Group (UK) Ltd, Croydon,
CRO 4YY

Pen & Sword Books Ltd incorporates the imprints of Pen & Sword
Archaeology, Atlas, Aviation, Battleground, Discovery, Family
History, History, Maritime, Military, Naval, Politics, Railways,
Select, Transport, True Crime, and Fiction, Frontline Books, Leo
Cooper, Praetorian Press, Seaforth Publishing and Wharncliffe.

For a complete list of Pen & Sword titles please contact
PEN & SWORD BOOKS LIMITED
47 Church Street, Barnsley, South Yorkshire, S70 2AS, England
E-mail: enquiries@pen-and-sword.co.uk
Website: www.pen-and-sword.co.uk

# Contents

# Preface

A voyage to an unfamiliar place can offer passengers the opportunity for exciting encounters. In 1599, for example, Thomas Dallam sailed to Turkey and visited a Greek island whose population had never gazed upon British people, and they flocked in droves to see him and his shipmates. At the other end of the time spectrum covered by this book, Jean Davies, brought up in rural Surrey, was delighted when she saw black people in Senegal in 1937 because she had never seen any before. Between these two extremes the passengers whose accounts are shared in this book experienced a great deal.

However, this book is concerned not with what passengers did or saw ashore, but with their experiences *at sea*. How has life on board ship changed for British passengers in the interval between Thomas Dallam's voyage and that taken by Jean Davies nearly 350 years later?

The best way to learn about the passenger experience is to hear what the passengers themselves had to say, so I have brought together a number of their accounts. They tell of dramatic storms and deaths, as well as the rather ordinary everyday activities that most passengers would have pursued on board ship. Taken together, their stories illustrate the evolution of the seagoing experience as revealed by those who experienced it.

Some of these accounts have never been published before – particularly those of Mary Perston, Herbert Watts, Mr and Mrs Hunt, and Jean Davies. It has also given me particular pleasure to unearth descriptions of voyages written by women, as the female point of view is so often neglected in maritime history. I have included accounts provided by different social classes as well: from the impoverished emigrants in steerage, to wealthy businessmen travelling first class. On occasion I have had to modernise spellings or punctuation to render their own words more readable.

Perhaps the most obvious changes for passengers over time lie in the technology employed by the ships in which they travelled. When passengers were dependent entirely on sail, their itineraries were subject to the vagaries of the wind. Henry Fielding took 44 days just to reach Portugal from London, simply because the wind stubbornly refused to blow in the right direction, and this experience was common. Sometimes there was too much wind, and many of our passengers describe storms forcing their ships to return to harbour for safety, being blown off course, getting lost, or suffering serious damage. Conversely, too little wind and a ship was becalmed – drifting aimlessly – sometimes for days on end.

Early steamships such as the SS *Great Western* continued to employ sails in addition to engines, but the advent of steam heralded a major change in the passenger experience. Ships were now faster and were much less affected by adverse weather conditions, so could therefore be scheduled to depart and arrive at set times. This meant that passengers could book in advance and not just take pot luck that a ship would leave on time or arrive when predicted. Engines evolved and became more efficient and more powerful, and the paddlewheels of early steamers were replaced by propellers so that speeds were greatly enhanced. The influence of technology can be seen by comparing the times for crossing of the Atlantic given by five of our passengers in this book. They each took different routes but the improved passage times are clear:

| Passengers | Ship | Year | Time to cross Atlantic |
|---|---|---|---|
| Pilgrim Fathers | *Mayflower*, 180 ton sailing ship | 1620 | 66 days |
| Janet Schaw | *Jamaica Packet*, 80 tons, brig | 1774 | 42 days |
| George Moore | SS *Great Western*, 1,700 tons, early paddlewheel steamship | 1844 | 14 days |
| Hubert Whitmarsh | RMS *Lucania*, 12,950 tons, triple expansion engines and two propellers | 1896 | 6 days |
| Percy Shaw Jeffrey | RMS *Empress of Scotland*, 24,581 tons, quadruple expansion engines and two propellers | 1926 | 4½ days |

This table also illustrates how ships have increased dramatically in size over time. More space allowed passengers to have bigger cabins. Mary Perston travelled first class by clipper in 1868 and still had to share a tiny cabin with a stranger she didn't like. Bigger ships meant passengers had privacy, and ship owners gradually began to appreciate that passengers would pay for luxury too – a wardrobe in the cabin, tasteful decor, running water, a properly sprung bed rather than a bunk. These improvements came thick and fast – electric lighting, heating, a shipboard library, swimming pools, shops, gyms and cinemas.

Without these amenities it can be hard to understand how passengers in earlier eras occupied their time, especially as voyages took so much longer than they do today. But although passengers had a more restricted range of entertainment in the past, they often enjoyed many of the things that sea travellers still appreciate in modern times.

Observing wildlife has been a constant source of pleasure to passengers in all eras. Whilst Mary Perston was pleased simply to see a cat on board to kill the rats in 1868, most passengers have taken more delight in watching dolphins, sharks, birds and schools of fish, amongst others, and this is a common subject about which our diarists write. A sunny, warm deck with a soft breeze is another pleasure that defies the ages, as is the delight of a sunset at sea which so many of the passengers in this book remark upon. Shipboard romances are also not new – something about the sea air can stir the passions, as Herbert Watts was surprised to discover in 1888. Other romantic feelings are hinted at by our shipboard diarists, but not confirmed in writing.

One particular experience that many passengers write about is the 'crossing the line' ceremony, where a member of the crew dresses as Neptune, king of the ocean, to welcome newcomers to his realm when they cross the equator for the first time. Jean Davies's account from 1937 is not very different to that described by other passengers in the preceding two centuries.

All the same, life onboard was sometimes very dull. Most of the sailing ship passengers described in this book were becalmed at some point, and even in the steamship era a vessel might endure unpleasantly hot latitudes for long periods, and both these eventualities were especially trying. Yet until the second half of the nineteenth century, ship owners made little effort to entertain or indulge their passengers. In 1844, George Moore struggled to keep his diary because he was so bored on the SS *Great Western*.

Soon enough, ship owners and crews realised that passengers could be a good commercial asset: they learned the value of providing enhanced passenger facilities and entertainments, and realised that people would pay for it. There were bigger, nicely decorated cabins, games, lounges, deckchairs, orchestras, sumptuous dining rooms, dances and concerts, as well as staff employed specifically to care for passengers' needs, such as stewards. Yet entertainment was not simply confined to the ship itself. When a ship docked at a foreign port, passengers have always been able to get off and look around, but the largely 'do-it-yourself' explorations that Herbert Watts or Maria Graham enjoyed in the nineteenth century were gradually replaced by the well-organised, bookable, guided tours that passengers such as the Hunts and the Jeffreys enjoyed in the twentieth century.

Meals were a particularly important part of the on-board experience and are discussed by most passengers in accounts of their voyages – especially when their food was wonderful, dreadful, or in short supply. In the era of sailing ships, travellers often had to provide their own provisions for the whole journey as the *Mayflower* passengers did, and on long voyages food or water could go off or be rationed, as both John Ovington and William Smith describe. Perhaps understandably the fixed times for eating on board often became the structure around which everything else happened in each 24-hour period. Once again ship owners gradually realised that passengers would pay for good quality meals and for the convenience of having food provided for them. Thus the twentieth century luxury ships, such as the *Lusitania*, were able to provide dining on a par with the very best restaurants ashore.

Another common theme taken up by passengers describing their experiences is sleep. Most of our diarists quickly found that they adapted to the unusual noises of life at sea and soon slept well despite the crew tramping the decks above their head, the shouting of orders or the clanking noise of the ship's propeller that kept poor Reverend Neville awake in 1858. Passengers are inclined to write about illness too – particularly seasickness which is so common and, like insomnia, can be induced by particularly rough motions of the ship. But there are more serious illnesses at sea: William Smith saw a frightening number of passengers and crew die of ship fever and dysentery in 1847, and Maria Graham watched her husband die in front of her in 1821 from an infection that may have been yellow fever. When an infectious disease takes hold on board ship there is nowhere to run. Other health risks for sea travellers over the centuries have included scurvy, which probably affected the *Mayflower* passengers, and infections such as malaria and cholera.

Additional threats to people travelling by sea included the ever-present problem of storms, as already alluded to. Many of the passengers in this book describe their cabins being flooded, and the sheer terror of a storm at sea. But violent weather could threaten the very existence of the ship: Janet Schaw's *Jamaica Packet* lost all its masts in a storm and at one point nearly sank, the *Mayflower*'s structural timbers were dangerously cracked mid-Atlantic, and storms caused the SS *London* to founder, taking all but three passengers to their deaths in 1866.

There were also dangers from other ships. Vessels often collided by accident on busy waterways, as Henry Fielding discovered in the eighteenth century, but some ships were a more deliberate threat. Thomas Dallam, for example, faced off privateers on board the *Hector* in 1599, whilst John Ovington escaped the attention not only of pirates but also of French warships during an international conflict. Phoebe Amory on board *Lusitania* was not so lucky in avoiding an enemy during wartime, yet although her ship was sunk by a U-boat's torpedo, she managed to escape with her life.

Historically, some of the other less welcome aspects of the passenger experience came, remarkably, from the crew and owners of the ship. We've come to expect a certain standard of customer service on a cruise these days, so it comes as something of a surprise to learn of owners defrauding their passengers, of rude or drunken sailors, rows between passengers and crew, and other goings-on. Yet during the early years of passenger transport, people were essentially carried on cargo ships with no more than basic accommodation – squeezed in amongst the crew and the freight – rather than in the purpose-built passenger ships of later eras. Passengers offered only a minor financial benefit compared to the huge profits that could be made from carrying cargo and so, to passengers' annoyance, sailings were often considerably delayed while lucrative cargo was awaited. The evolution of steamships, however, with their regular sailing schedules forced owners and captains to stick to the advertised times of departure. The quality of the passenger experience was also determined, at least in part, by the class of travel booked, and Hubert Whitmarsh describes the rude and thoughtless treatment of third class or 'steerage' passengers in 1896.

Finally, across the time period covered by this book, it is notable that the function of the ship itself has changed. In the days of sail, most passengers travelled to emigrate, or for family or business reasons. So the ship was often merely the laborious means by which a person went from A to B; it was slow, uncomfortable, boring, and occasionally dangerous but it had to be endured because there was no other way to travel and passengers made the best of it. However, by the time that Percy Shaw Jeffrey took his world cruise in 1926, the ship was just as much a vital and desirable part of his travel experience as the numerous exotic locations he visited. He and his wife were not travelling out of necessity, they were on holiday, and their ship was a floating luxury hotel.

It is fascinating – and occasionally shocking – to explore the lives of passengers afloat in the past. Whether they were at sea for a few days or many months, they all have a tale to tell. I hope you enjoy reading about their experiences in this book, and that by the end you will appreciate how our travelling experience in the twenty-first century is very much improved compared to that of our ancestors.

*Chapter One*

# A Queen's Gift for the Sultan

## *(1599, Thomas Dallam, Hector)*

Thomas Dallam was an organ builder from Lancashire. In the late 1590s he was commanded by Queen Elizabeth I to take an organ as a gift to Sultan Mehmed III of the Ottoman Empire. Elizabeth recognised the Sultan as a possible military ally but also desired trade with his citizens in the Levant and so sent merchants to accompany the organ as a trading envoy.

The organ was demonstrated to the Queen, then disassembled and packed for transport to the Ottoman court in Constantinople (modern Istanbul). British state papers recorded this gift: 'A great and curious present is going to the Grand Turk, which will scandalise other nations especially the Germans'.

The Ottoman Empire seemed an exotic world a long way from England, with a colourful and powerful ruler. Yet Dallam was not a merchant, soldier, diplomat, or even a sailor, and so not the type of person who would normally undertake such a long voyage. This was unusual, and helps to explain why he wrote a journal describing his adventures.

### Leaving England

Passenger travel was novel enough for Dallam to delight in describing all the details of his travelling experience. For example, he was uncertain about how much clothing to pack so decided to take the following items: two suits, two waistcoats, one hat, nine shirts, two pairs of breeches, one pair of garters, five items of footwear, two pairs of stockings, one pair of gloves, one gown, and 12 handkerchiefs. Although he took some food, Dallam was not expected to provision himself since he was travelling on the Queen's business, but he did take his own bedding.

On Friday, 9 February 1599, Dallam was rowed from London to Gravesend by Thames watermen. They operated as 'river taxis' – ferrying people up and down the waterway to board ships, attend social events and so forth. On reaching the *Hector*, Dallam checked his luggage had arrived. He had been permitted to bring an early piano-like instrument – called a virginal – so that he might practise his keyboard skills at sea.

No cabins had yet been appointed for passengers, so Dallam spent four days at an inn until the *Hector* was ready to sail. The ship soon reached Deal but had to anchor there because the wind was against them. Sailing ships were at the mercy of the wind: too little and progress was slow, too much and they could be damaged. Yet the commonest problem was often simply that the wind was blowing in the wrong direction – a 'contrary wind'. A sailing ship could not sail into a wind blowing from the direction in which it wished to travel. Hence the southerly wind would not allow the *Hector* to progress from Deal towards Dover. And there they stayed, trapped, for four days.

On the fourth evening, Dallam and colleagues went ashore to 'make ourselves merry' but in the middle of the night they were ordered back to the *Hector* as the wind had suddenly become favourable – a 'fair wind'. One trumpeter was so drunk that they had to leave him behind, yet now they could sail for Dover and make their way westwards along 'The Sleeve' as the English Channel was then known (a literal translation of the French *La Manche*).

After about 90 miles, the wind turned contrary once more and blew up into a 'marvellous great storm for the space of eight and forty hours'. During this fierce weather they lost touch with their pinnace, the *Lanerett*, which had been following behind, and once the storm abated, the crew and passengers on the *Hector* found themselves lost in fog. The crew reckoned they were somewhere off the Channel Islands but the fog continued for another day so no-one could be sure. The ship sailed on blindly: their inability to see either stars or sun meant that accurate navigation was impossible. Then, unexpectedly, imminent disaster loomed up at them from out of the fog:

'Upon a sudden, we saw the sea break against the shore and on the which was very great rocks, and we were so near the shore that it was not possible to cast about in time to save ourselves from shipwreck.

But it pleased almighty God so to defend us from harm that we were just before the harbour at Dartmouth, a very straight entry betwixt these great rocks that are on both sides of that entry'.

The *Hector* escaped into Dartmouth away from the weather, and stayed there four days.

## The Danger of Privateers

While in port, envoys were sent out to local seaside towns to try and locate the *Lanerett*. They soon discovered that the pinnace had been chased by a fleet of Channel privateers called Dunkirkers. These ships operated from the Spanish Netherlands, especially the port of Dunkirk, under the authority of the Spanish crown. They were raiders who attacked enemy shipping for commercial gain – especially Dutch and English vessels – and it was a very profitable business.

Captured ships and their cargoes were sold but their crews and passengers could be dealt with very harshly and even killed. To avoid being taken, the crew of the *Lanerett* had run the vessel ashore at Falmouth; the pinnace had lost her topmast but was repaired and her crew sent a message to the *Hector* that they should rendezvous at Plymouth.

After their reunion, another change in wind direction trapped *Hector* and *Lanerett* in the harbour for a week. Eventually the wind blew in their favour, but a caravel entering port made an urgent appeal to communicate by sounding a trumpet. Two men came on board and told a frightening tale. They and four other men were all that remained of the crew of the *Plough* that had been captured by seven Dunkirkers. The privateers interrogated them about the *Hector* and its sailing schedule but although they had not known anything, many had been put to death in an attempt to make them talk.

The survivors advised the master of the *Hector*, Richard Parsons, not to sail without greater protection. However, the redoubtable captain refused. His ship was well-armed, he was on the Queen's business and already frustrated by the delays that had beset them. Consequently, the *Hector* and *Lanerett* were soon under way once more.

The two ships made excellent progress under a fair wind, but the next morning the lookout at the top of the mainmast sang out that there were three ships in sight, and within a short while this became seven. The Dunkirkers! The captain ordered the *Hector* to get ready for battle: the gunners prepared the cannon and every man took up his musket.

Although the *Hector* was running ahead of the privateers 'our captain thought it not fit to show ourselves fearful or cowardly' and so he altered course to intercept the Dunkirkers. The *Hector* was large, heavily-armed and fast, and Captain Parsons predicted that chasing the privateers would persuade them that *Hector* was a warship. In this era, naval vessels were not always easily discernible from non-military ships, and neither officers nor crew wore a uniform.

The ruse worked amazingly well. The Dunkirkers turned tail and fled. Yet to maintain credibility, the *Hector* had to persist with the chase and within half an hour had caught up with them. After a few warning shots, the privateers were ordered to heave to, and to send their commanders over in a boat.

The *Hector*'s captain could not afford the manpower to sail seven captured privateers back to Plymouth as prizes: without putting some of his own men on board each ship they could simply sneak away at nightfall, or change their minds and attack him. He pretended to believe assurances from the privateers' commanders that they were simply merchant ships and he let them go. The crew were unhappy about this because they believed they had lost considerable prize money – Dallam even suggests that the captain had been handsomely bribed by the privateer commanders to release them – but whatever his methods, Captain Parsons had cleverly ensured they could continue with the Queen's mission unmolested.

## Mediterranean

For a few days, the *Hector* and *Lanerett* made good progress along the coast of France and Spain. Then, somewhere off the coast of Portugal, the wind suddenly died away for four days and they were becalmed. Yet Dallam enjoyed watching 'an infinite company of porpoises about our ship' and then: 'We saw two or three great monstrous fishes or whales, the which did spout water up into the air, like as smoke doth ascend out of a chimney. Sometimes we might see a great part of their body above the water'.

On 27 March the wind picked up again and this carried them into the Mediterranean and away from the sphere of operation of the Dunkirkers. As they sailed through, Dallam admired the strong, highly-fortified Spanish town of Gibraltar which would not yet fall to the British for over 100 years.

To Dallam, unaccustomed to being so far south, it was 'exceedingly hot' but thankfully the wind kept the ship moving eastwards. On 30 March, the *Hector* and *Lanerett* entered the harbour at Algiers: Dallam would not be the last to remark on the beauty of this white city from the sea.

Things got off to a bad start here when Captain Parsons was arrested for refusing to show the Queen's gift to the local King. In some fear for his own safety, Dallam had to go and explain that it had been dismantled and the captain was then released and given a present of two bulls and three sheep as an apology!

Returning aboard, Captain Parsons agreed to take a party of Turks as passengers to Scandaroon (modern Iskenderun in Turkey). This was part of the *Hector*'s route since it had cargo to deliver there, and no doubt the passengers paid well. There were no regularly scheduled ship departures for long distance voyages, so passengers had to await a ship sailing in the right direction and then negotiate a fare with the captain, if he was willing to take them. Quite often, passengers would break their journey into a series of 'legs', stopping at intermediate ports where they would seek another ship to carry them closer to their final destination. Accommodation on vessels that accepted these 'spur of the moment' passengers was usually primitive.

On 4 April they left Algiers and sailed along the north coast of Africa. Here they witnessed the intense lightning that sometimes occurs in hot climates, but which Dallam had not seen before:

'We saw very strange lightning in the sky, or in the air. It was very wonderful and strange, for we might see the air open and a fire like a very hot iron taken out of a smith's forge: sometimes in likeness of a running worm, another time like a horseshoe, and again like a leg and a foot. Also the thunder claps were also exceedingly great.'

They headed to Tunis, then bore north-eastwards, and by 14 April were off the coast of Sicily where they witnessed flashing fires from the volcano at night. On the way to Malta, they intercepted a ship heavily laden with an expensive cargo. Again the *Hector*'s captain did not take her as a prize. The ship came from a port under the control of the Ottomans (Chios, in Greece) and, clearly, capturing one of the Sultan's ships on the way to a meeting with him would have been poor diplomacy. Yet Dallam preferred to believe Captain Parsons had once again taken a bribe.

The ships stopped at the island of Zante (modern Zakynthos) on 20 April for provisions but had to wait six days for health clearance. The Ionian islands were governed by Venice and any ship without a bill of health was detained under observation before anyone was allowed to disembark, to prevent the spread of contagion. It must have been very dull, trapped on board a small ship in the heat for six days, with nothing but the same company and the same view.

An educated man like Dallam could read, but books were expensive and so he was unlikely to own many. Card and dice games were popular pursuits, and of course Dallam had his diary to maintain and his virginal to play. The *Hector* carried a preacher, so on Sundays there was divine service. During their quarantine, Dallam planned his investigation of the island and set off eagerly with two companions as soon as he could; he particularly enjoyed exploring the mysteries of the Greek Orthodox Church, which was so different to the Christianity he knew at home.

The Turkish passengers agitated for the *Hector* to depart as soon as possible, and so on 2 May the ships resumed their voyage. They weaved between the Greek islands – Cythera, Crete, Milos, Karpathos – and Dallam shares some of the local mythology with his readers: Helen of Troy was born on Cythera; an enchanted brass statue on Crete prevented storms. In the sixteenth century, magic and myth were taken very seriously, or at least more readily accepted at face value. Many mariners believed in the existence of sea monsters: for example, in 1583, the explorer Sir Humphrey Gilbert reported a monster with 'long teeth and glaring eyes' and 'bellowing as doth a lion'.

After a couple of days becalmed, the crew sighted Cyprus and on 12 May dropped off a passenger who had boarded at Zakynthos. They sighted Mount Lebanon as they continued their journey, and soon were at anchor off Iskenderun where Dallam and some of the crew went ashore to hunt for hogs and wildfowl in the interior. Yet they found the thick woods difficult to negotiate and narrowly escaped being ambushed by a large group of armed locals.

Their Turkish passengers disembarked, but on 18 May a large contingent of Ottoman troops arrived. Local merchants urged Captain Parsons not to unload his cargo because the soldiers would pillage it. Unfortunately, as soon as one division left another would arrive, so the *Hector* was forced to wait a frustrating 12 days until they had all departed. Only then could the cargo be unloaded.

Communications in the sixteenth century were slow, so Dallam marvelled that traders used pigeons to communicate speedily between Iskenderun and Aleppo, where the cargo was bound. A message reached its destination in four hours, even though the cities were 70 miles apart.

While in Iskenderun, the captain organised a regular boat trip to Tarsus to visit the market there, so that they might keep the ship's provisions topped up. It was essential to do this as unexpected delays at sea might otherwise force rationing of food and water. The *Hector* had a crew, merchants and passengers all to be fed and accommodated, but had limited room to store food and water once the space occupied by the cargo and the people was taken into account. This meant that supplies had to be constantly topped up at every opportunity.

Dallam and some crew members went picking samphire on the rocks at the harbour's mouth near to where, he was told, Jonah had been disgorged from the stomach of the whale. Samphire was eaten commonly as a salad.

## Bound for Constantinople

On 20 June, the *Hector* and *Lanerett* set sail for their final destination: Constantinople. Their route took them along the southern coast of modern Turkey, which Dallam called 'Asia the Less', until six days later they reached Rhodes. Here, the author notes, 'this day died one Thomas Cable, who was under 20 years of age, and son to one of the owners of our ship'. Two other young men were also to die in the ensuing month. Dallam does not record the cause of their deaths, but scurvy is one possibility because we now know that on long voyages an absence of fresh fruit and vegetables caused vitamin C deficiency.

Having an unfavourable wind, the *Hector* anchored at the northern tip of Rhodes and the captain replenished his provisions once again. Dallam and companions set off to explore the town but an unfortunate incident saw the ship's preacher and a colleague arrested and threatened with a public whipping. This happened because the captain had not given a gift to the town's deputy leader, as was expected. Fortunately, the oversight was quickly corrected and the *Hector*'s passengers released.

The ships passed into the Aegean and cruised amongst its many small islands. They anchored off Samos and were delayed a few days by unfavourable winds, so men went ashore for firewood and water. On the evening of 10 July, as the *Hector* was put about in the gathering darkness, it ran aground, much to the consternation of everyone on board. Captain Parsons blamed the leadsman who had been asked to sound the depth of the water.

After a great deal of nocturnal anguish the ship was eventually floated off again by morning. But this was not the end of their troubles. At dawn they spied four galleys and a frigate behaving suspiciously. It was clear that they had their eyes on the *Hector* – pirates probably – but the captain bluffed again. He assembled everyone onto the main deck and asked that they 'make as great a show as we could' and as the *Hector* passed the threatening ships, he ordered all five trumpets to be sounded loudly. This bravado worked, and once again the ships continued on their way.

By 15 July, the ship's food supplies were running low once more and its drinking water had become contaminated: 'We had nothing to eat but rice boiled in stinking water, and our beverages did also stink'. The drinking water on ships became contaminated with the taste of the oak puncheons it was stored in, and other things such as dead insects and scraps of food. Consequently, and particularly in a hot climate, it stagnated and grew algae and bacteria. Where possible, it was preferable to drink beer, wine, or rum since the alcohol content tended to keep them sweet-tasting.

Before disembarking at the island of Chios, Parsons cautioned Dallam that he should not take even the tiniest amount of any of the crops grown locally – grapes, mastic and cotton – as if caught he would be imprisoned. He further warned that if Dallam did not return on time, he would sail without him. Much to Dallam's surprise, the *Hector*'s landing party became a great centre of attention, since the islanders had never seen British people before. Intrigued, they flocked to view them in great numbers, even climbing up on a wall to get a better view and causing it to collapse. Unfortunately, though, they obtained no significant supplies.

The ships headed for Tenedos, but it was a slow journey with an initial contrary wind, followed by a becalming. They reached the island on 19 July where Dallam could see the ruins of ancient Troy on the mainland. During the days which followed, a running comedy ensued. As they neared their final destination, Turkish ships hailed them, and their captains wished to come on board. However, the *Hector*'s captain was aware of the custom that a Turk coming on board ship expected a gift, yet he had nothing to give them. Thus every time they sighted Turkish ships, the *Hector* up-anchored and sailed hastily away.

This couldn't last forever, and eventually they were obliged to halt for a Turkish galley which sent over a boat demanding a present for both the galley's captain and the admiral of the fleet. Poor Captain Parsons hunted high and low and eventually unearthed two chests for the admiral and some pipes and tobacco for the galley's captain. Smoking was then still something of a novelty.

Meanwhile Dallam and friends went ashore and managed to get some provisions. They also explored some of the ruins of Troy but like many future passengers on a shore excursion, he wanted to find a souvenir to take home:

'There we saw more at large the ruins of the walls and houses of Troy, and from thence I brought a piece of a white marble pillar, the which I broke with my own hands, having a good hammer which my mate Harvey did carry ashore for the same purpose. And I brought this piece of marble to London'.

On 23 July, the ships reached the Hellespont (modern Dardanelles), the stretch of water that connected the Aegean to the Sea of Marmara. The city of Constantinople sat on the coast of this inland sea. Adverse winds prevented their initial progress, but the British ambassador in Constantinople heard of their plight and sent a ship rowed by slaves to take some of the passengers off the *Hector* and carry them down to the city.

Dallam reached Constantinople on 15 August. It had taken him an astounding 183 days since leaving London to reach his destination. The *Hector* arrived one day later and on 17 August, Dallam and his associates began unloading the Sultan's present from the Queen. Unfortunately, when they sat down to reconstruct the organ, Dallam realised with horror that prolonged storage in the hot ship's hold had caused all the glue to decay and that the rolling of cargo during heavy weather had 'bruised and broken' many of the organ's pipes.

It took 15 days to repair the damage and to reassemble the organ, but the Sultan did not receive his gift until 25 September. Dallam set up the organ to strike the hour and then play a few tunes automatically; he was then invited into court to play for the Sultan and his enormous entourage. Fortunately, after such an appallingly long journey, the concert was a great success. He was even offered two wives if he would stay but Dallam returned to England in 1600 where he married and became the progenitor of a renowned family of organ builders.

*Chapter Two*

# Early Emigrants to America

## *(1620, William Bradford, Mayflower)*

It is no exaggeration to say that emigration to America in the early seventeenth century was a dangerous business. The voyage alone was long, gruelling and hazard-ridden. Many passengers on the *Mayflower* in 1620 knew the fate of an earlier emigrant ship, the *William & Thomas*, which had made the Atlantic crossing the year before, under the leadership of a dissenter, Francis Blackwell. An agent for many of the passengers, Robert Cushman, described the outcome of that voyage in a letter:

'Master Blackwell's ship came not there till March [1619]. But going, towards winter [1618], they had still northwest winds which carried them to the southward, beyond their course. And the master of the ship and some six of the mariners dying, it seemed they could not find the [Chesapeake] Bay till after long seeking and beating about.

'Master Blackwell is dead, and Master Maggner the captain. Yea, there are dead... 130 persons, one and [an]other, in that ship. It is said, there were in all 180 persons in the ship, so as they were packed together like herrings. They had amongst them the flux [dysentery], and also want of fresh water; so as it is here rather wondered at that so many are alive, than that so many are dead.'

Even if they survived the voyage, the living conditions at the final destination were tough: many of the settlers of the first significant British colony, Jamestown, established in 1607, had starved to death; there was disease, and there had been fights with the native American tribes. Population statistics tell a stark tale. From December 1606 to May 1618, around 1,800 people set sail from England to Virginia. Of these, about 100 returned home, about

1,100 died en route or in Virginia, and only 600 were still living in Virginia according to the 1618 census.

So it took a certain amount of bravery – or desperation – to face the prospect of crossing the Atlantic to establish a new colony. The majority of the *Mayflower*'s passengers were dissenters, a Christian group with significantly different views to the Church of England, at a time when non-Anglican worship was illegal in Britain. However, since many of the passengers were not dissenters, religious freedom was not the sole inspiration for emigration. Britain at this time was an impoverished, unequal, intolerant society that offered most people little prospect for improving their personal circumstances. A chance to start again and create a new community was thus appealing. The strength of determination for change amongst dissenter and non-dissenter alike is demonstrated by the fact that they came aboard as families. There were children and servants; three wives were already pregnant; two families even brought their pet dog.

William Bradford was one of the dissenters. He had been born to a farming family in Austerfield, Yorkshire in 1596, and much later became a governor of the Plymouth Colony in America. It is owing to his account that details of the voyage of the *Mayflower* have survived.

## A False Start

On 5 August 1620, Bradford and his fellow passengers were in Southampton. They had already experienced delays while finalising their arrangements, and so the window of opportunity for safe passage across the Atlantic before the autumn and winter gales was beginning to close. They walked through Southampton's West Gate to board, not one but two sailing ships bound for America – the *Mayflower*, and the smaller *Speedwell*. In this era there were no purpose-built long distance passenger vessels, so both would have been cargo ships hurriedly converted to carry people. Even after this conversion, the living quarters for each passenger during the voyage were probably created simply by using wooden or canvas screens to divide up the space below the main deck, which would have offered families only a modicum of privacy.

Every passenger discovered immediately that it was all very cramped; on the *Mayflower* each person's berth was less than the size of a modern single bed. This small space had to house their mattress, which passengers provided themselves, and a trunk or bag holding all their possessions and clothing needed during the voyage. Mattresses were most likely made of straw and probably laid directly onto the bare wooden decks, with passengers also supplying their own pillows and blankets.

The voyage did not start well. Shortly after leaving Southampton, *Speedwell* sprang a leak in the English Channel and both ships tied up at Dartmouth for ten days while the smaller vessel was repaired. Setting sail once more, *Speedwell*'s leak returned when the ships entered the Atlantic and they were again forced back to Dartmouth. This time it was decided to leave the apparently unseaworthy *Speedwell* and some of her passengers behind, and *Mayflower* finally departed from Plymouth on 6 September 1620. The *Mayflower* was not large – perhaps around 100 feet long, and with a capacity of about 180 tons – but she carried 102 passengers.

Not only did the emigrants have to provide their own bedding, they also supplied their own food for the voyage, as well as sufficient rations to sustain them over winter in America while they learned to survive off the land. To this end, the settlers took with them equipment such as woodworking tools, agricultural implements, cooking utensils and weapons with which to both hunt and defend themselves. So this small ship carried a large and varied cargo.

## The Voyage Begins

The captain of the *Mayflower* was Christopher Jones. Previously, his main experience had been in taking cargo to continental Europe, and although he had never crossed the Atlantic, his first mate and pilot had both done so. Yet Jones had been in command of the *Mayflower* for at least 11 years and, aged 50, was a seasoned mariner with perhaps 25 years' experience as a ship's master. No doubt he was as relieved as anyone to be finally under way.

Despite their earlier setbacks, *Mayflower* made good headway for a few days with a fair wind, yet many of the passengers were badly afflicted with seasickness once they entered the ocean. To add to their misery, a young crew member decided to mock them, as Bradford notes in his account:

'There was a proud and very profane young man, one of the seamen, of a lusty, able body, which made him the more haughty. He would always be condemning the poor people in their sickness, and cursing them daily with grievous execrations, and did not let to tell them that he hoped to help to cast half of them overboard before they came to their journey's end, and to make merry with what they had. And if he were by any gently reproved, he would curse and swear most bitterly.'

Maintaining order on a merchant ship was not always easy. Although the captain's word was held to be law, it was not necessarily appropriate for him to be a strict disciplinarian. Seamen were paid employees hired for one voyage at a time, and so captains were generally loath to dish out the brutal discipline of the Royal Navy where men were flogged, imprisoned, beaten, starved or worse. Captains with a brutal reputation might find it hard to obtain future commands and harder still to find a crew. Captain Jones knew he depended on his men giving their best during a long voyage, and not deserting when they reached Massachusetts where he might otherwise be left stranded. He was therefore probably reluctant to intervene in any unpleasant goings-on between passengers and crew. Besides, seamen swore and got up to mischief all the time and they were not going to stop just because there were devout Christians on board.

Nonetheless, it is with some satisfaction that Bradford later records that the young seaman who had so taunted them was a few weeks later smitten 'with a grievous disease, of which he died in a desperate manner'. He writes that despite the young man's insistence that he would be throwing dead passengers overboard during the voyage, the seaman himself was the first to be pitched over the side. Bradford and his fellow passengers viewed his death as the 'just hand of God'.

Many of the diseases that attacked seafarers particularly were infectious, such as typhus and dysentery, and this was clearly not the cause of the young sailor's death as no-one else suffered. It might have been gangrene after an injury on board, or perhaps appendicitis or a chest infection, but scurvy is another possibility as it affected seamen who lived off a ship's diet for prolonged periods. Scurvy, as described earlier, is caused by vitamin C deficiency, and sufferers could become delirious as they neared their end.

In the seventeenth century, food on a lengthy voyage was extremely limited in its variety. A captain might order some fresh provisions to last for the first few days of the trip, such as vegetables or bread, but for the bulk of a long journey people had to live off dried food that could be stored for prolonged periods without deteriorating. The *Mayflower*'s passengers would have purchased salted meat or fish, cereals such as oatmeal, dried peas and beans, raisins perhaps, and the ubiquitous sea-goer's fare of ship's biscuits or 'hard tack' – hard-baked round cakes made from cereals, and usually filled with maggots. The settlers also brought with them butter, cheese, oil, and various herbs and spices. The ship carried drinking water, but passengers and crew alike would have consumed beer in preference because it kept and tasted better.

The main cooking facility on board was the small stove in the ship's galley, intended primarily for the crew, but passengers could also light their own small fires for cooking in sand-filled trays called fireboxes. With so many passengers and so little space, they had to be organised to ensure that everyone had access to a hot meal during the day. Cooking made the dried provisions more appetising, but was not allowed during storms because of the danger of a ship-wide fire. Everyone had to be constantly vigilant against the outbreak of fire since all heat and light came from naked flames, and many of the crew and passengers would also have smoked tobacco. Yet the ship was made of wood with highly flammable rigging and caulking soaked in pitch, so once a fire caught hold it was practically impossible to put out.

The voyage was an uncomfortable experience. The passenger quarters were on the *Mayflower*'s 'tween deck, the middle layer between the main deck, where the crew worked the ship, and the hold, the lowermost space which was crammed full of stores. The passengers slept on this 'tween deck, and although they could come on deck in fine weather, during a storm they were confined below. It was a dark, damp, smelly and airless space with insufficient headroom for an adult to stand up straight. It became increasingly cold, too, as autumn unfolded.

The passengers' discomfort would have been magnified by leakage of seawater from the deck above. Gaps between the ship's timbers were filled by packing them with resin-soaked hemp fibres and then sealing them with pitch, but it was an imperfect process because ship's timbers moved during a voyage as the hull was twisted by the sea, and there was rarely time to effect ongoing repairs. So the ceiling of the 'tween deck would have leaked, particularly during storms when the main deck above the passengers was repeatedly awash with seawater.

For toilets, passengers used a bucket or potty. The crew used 'heads' cut in the ship's bows, but they were not very private and difficult for landsmen to access unless the sea was calm.

During good weather the monotony of life at sea must have been difficult to contend with. The *Mayflower* was at sea for many weeks once it finally left England, and the passengers had to fill their time as best they could. No doubt women engaged themselves in fulfilling some of the traditionally female duties of the period such as cooking, sewing and caring for the children. Men would have spent time planning their settlement of America, and those who were educated probably read books by candlelight, on subjects such as building and agriculture to acquire new knowledge. The dissenters would have enjoyed plenty of religious debate, worship and studying of the Bible throughout the week, but on British ships the captain often led religious observance on a Sunday.

## Stormy Seas

Storms beset the *Mayflower* constantly during the second half of her Atlantic crossing. Bradford recounts that 'they were encountered many times with cross winds, and met with many fierce storms, with which the ship was shrewdly shaken'. This was not unexpected because the *Mayflower*'s delayed departure meant crossing the ocean in the autumn and early winter when Atlantic storms were more common.

Research with a replica of the *Mayflower* in the 1950s showed that she could make 7½ knots with a following wind but adverse weather could negate this good progress. In the fiercest storms, a captain was forced to take in all the sails, or lose them, and allow the ship to ride the seas 'a-hull' or 'under bare poles'. The ship was then at the mercy of the storm as far as its direction of travel was concerned and was often blown many miles off course. Bradford recollects that sometimes this situation endured for many days at a time. Once the storm had passed, the captain then had to find his new position and plot a course using primitive instruments such as a compass, and a cross-staff or quadrant to determine latitude. Longitude could not be determined at this time so captains were never able to plot their precise position.

The storms must have been truly frightening for the passengers. They would have been tossed around with their belongings in the cramped darkness below decks, wondering if they would make it through alive and if they'd be able to get out quickly enough if the ship began to sink. Not that escaping a wreck offered any hope of survival – oceanic travel was in its infancy, so if the *Mayflower* went down in the vast expanse of the Atlantic, there was precious little chance of rescue by another ship.

During one storm, the *Mayflower* suffered major structural damage. Bradford describes how 'one of the main beams in the midships was bowed and cracked, which put them in some fear that the ship could not be able to perform the voyage'. After intense discussions between crew and passengers, it was decided to use a screw jack to raise the beam, then prop it up with a post. This seems to have reassured everyone that the ship was strong enough to proceed.

Yet there were other potential dangers from what Bradford describes as a 'long beating at sea'. In one gale, a young passenger called John Howland came up on deck but the sea suddenly bucked the *Mayflower* violently beneath his feet and threw him over the side. Bradford explains what happened next:

'But it pleased God that he caught hold of the topsail halyards, which hung overboard and ran out at length, yet he held his hold (though he was sundry fathoms under water) till he was hauled up by the same rope to the brim of the water, and then with a boat hook and other means got into the ship again and his life saved. And though he was something ill with it, yet he lived many years after.'

John Howland's survival was fortunate, but not just on his own account. Many people who are descended from him owe their existence to his tenacious grabbing of that ship's rope, including US President Franklin D. Roosevelt. Only one passenger died on the voyage. A young servant called William Butten expired from unknown causes on 6 November. However, a new passenger also arrived during the voyage in the form of a baby boy, born on board to Stephen and Elizabeth Hopkins – the appropriately named Oceanus.

Three days after William Butten died, land was sighted and it proved to be Cape Cod in Massachusetts; at this, Bradford recalls that 'they were not a little joyful'. After some difficult manoeuvring of the ship on an unfamiliar shore with presumably no charts to guide them – or at best very primitive ones – the *Mayflower* eventually anchored in the harbour at Cape Cod on 11 November 1620.

It had taken 66 days for the *Mayflower*'s passengers to reach America, at an abysmally slow average speed of two miles per hour. That same transatlantic distance is now covered in less than eight hours by commercial airlines. Remarkably, it took over 250 years from the time of the *Mayflower*'s voyage before this journey could be done in less than a week by sea.

Yet the colonists' transatlantic voyage was only the beginnings of their hardships. The harsh American winter and their weakened state due to malnutrition, scurvy and lack of exercise, forced them to stay aboard the *Mayflower* until January while they built a suitable refuge on land. Unhappily, by the end of the first winter, 45 of their number had died.

*Chapter Three*

# Voyage to India

## *(1689, John Ovington, Benjamin)*

Thirty-six-year-old Yorkshireman, John Ovington, boarded the ship *Benjamin*, bound for India, part of what was then known as the East Indies. An Anglican minister, Ovington had been employed by the East India Company to look after the spiritual needs of employees at its 'factory', or trading station, in Surat on the west coast of India for which he would be paid £50 per year. The ship was owned by his employer and he was also required to function as its chaplain during the voyage.

### Pirates and the French

At 430 tons, the *Benjamin* was considerably more than twice the size of the *Mayflower* and was only 12 months old. The crew of 90 men was commanded by Captain Leonard Browne, and although principally a trading vessel, the *Benjamin* was also transporting 24 passengers. The ship was well armed, sporting 30 cannon, since it would sail through waters infested with pirates, and an unarmed merchant ship carrying thousands of pounds worth of cargo would otherwise be an easy target. But pirates were not the only danger – Britain was in a Grand Alliance against France in the Nine Years' War, and so French warships were a potential threat as well.

The *Benjamin* was loaded with cargo, provisions and passengers at Gravesend, then on 11 April 1689 set sail in company with a number of others, as a convoy offered greater protection. It was a memorable date since the new Protestant monarchs William III and Mary II were being crowned at Westminster Abbey on that day.

The ships passed through the Downs off the east coast of Kent before entering the English Channel and cruising its length. But this uneventful passage was suddenly interrupted:

'We had not long left the Land's End of England, before we espied a great fleet of ships which appeared to us at a distance like a floating forest, and seized us with no little consternation. Their lying off not far from Brest, made us for some time conjecture them to be French, till we were happily undeceived by the approach of an English frigate which discovered them to be friends.'

Nevertheless, the threat of enemy action proved too much for the crew of one vessel in the convoy, which took one look at the 'French' fleet and fled. The remaining ships took advantage of a favourable wind and peacefully negotiated the Bay of Biscay and the Iberian Peninsula to reach the Portuguese island of Madeira. The *Benjamin* was inspected by local inquisitors who checked the vessel for 'sickness or other objection that might hinder the liberty of traffic', and only when it was pronounced free of contagion could anyone step ashore.

Here the *Benjamin* was re-provisioned, especially with fruits and wine. The ample food, drink and beautiful climate tempted some crewmen to desert, although Ovington believed they were lured away to join the Catholic faith by local Jesuits. Captain Browne also believed this for he captured two local priests, threatening to enlist them to replace his seamen, until the resultant uproar forced him to back down. Yet there was a fortunate outcome from this dispute: the *Benjamin* departed rapidly without due ceremony and thus avoided two French warships which arrived shortly afterwards. Learning of the English convoy, they set off in hot pursuit but fortunately headed in the wrong direction.

## Nature's Threats and Charms

On the way to the Cape Verde Islands, Ovington wondered at the marine wildlife he saw:

'In our way we were entertained with an unusual prospect – which to fresh navigators was very divertive – which was several winged fish which took flight in the air while their fins were moist, but dropped into the ocean as soon as they grew dry and thereby inactive... When they drop into the ocean, the watchful dolphins are generally ready to devour them.'

The ship was also subjected to a frightening tornado – an intense storm that seemed to come from nowhere. The weather had been sedate and temperate for many hours, and then suddenly, within a quarter of an hour, the skies changed and there was a surprisingly violent storm of rain and wind. Without the careful and speedy handling of the ship by the crew, Ovington was in no doubt that the *Benjamin* could have been endangered. Fortunately, the storm dissipated as quickly as it had arisen. During storms the rainwater was collected and used to top up the *Benjamin*'s stocks of drinking water.

Captain Browne anchored the ship at Praia harbour, Santiago, the largest of the Cape Verde islands. It was fortunate they arrived when they did for a second fierce storm accosted them that very night. This one was 'so outrageous that the ship dragged her anchor, and our ruin had been inevitable had it been much fiercer': they were anchored so close inshore that the *Benjamin* was in danger of being propelled landwards and wrecked.

Santiago was, disappointingly, unable to supply them with provisions. Ovington, though not impressed by the islanders' reputation for thieving and prostitution, was intrigued by the sulphurous clouds from the volcano on the nearby island of Fogo. Its eruptions sent pumice stones cascading into the sea and Ovington examined some as they floated about the ship.

Shortly after leaving these islands, heading south, the *Benjamin* found the trade winds. These 'constant gentle gales' ensured that the sailors did not need to handle even a sail for days on end. The pleasant weather was very enjoyable and helped relieve the monotony of the voyage, since everyone was able to relax and relish the life afloat in the sweet, warm climate.

During this glorious weather, Ovington took great interest in leaning over the side to observe the many different species of fish in the clear water as the ship sped along. He watched as the sailors caught sharks and porpoises, hauling them aboard to kill and eat. But that wasn't all:

'Several dolphins followed our ship, which surpass all the creatures of the watery element in beauty and a quick fin, and is therefore called the Arrow of the Sea. They shine the brightest, and swim the fastest, of any fish in the ocean... The flesh of it is white and delicate, which when larded and roasted fresh, no Roman dainties or eastern luxury can out-vie the grateful food.

We met likewise with shoals of albacores... and with multitudes of bonitos [tuna-like fish], which are named for their goodness and excellence for eating, so that sometimes for more than twenty days the whole ship's company have feasted on these curious fish.'

As the *Benjamin* approached the equator, the sails flapped as the wind died away. The 'face of the ocean was as smooth as that of a crystal mirror', says Ovington poetically. Yet the heat below decks, particularly below the water line where little air circulated, was stifling. The ship's supply of fresh water was stored here and was soon 'full of small worms' and any items of polished steel such as a sword quickly became tarnished or rusted in the 'constant brooding heat'.

## Problems with Water

They sighted land shortly after crossing the equator – the island of Annobon which lies off modern-day Equatorial Guinea. Regrettably they had to wait two days for a favourable wind before they could dock, but in the meantime the natives rowed out to them with supplies of oranges and chickens which were much appreciated as their stores were almost spent.

Continuing south they eventually sighted the African coast near the Congo estuary, but as they neared shore they were becalmed. Their rations at this stage were meagre and rapidly deteriorating: 'The provisions being salt beef and the water in the cask so unsavoury and corrupt that to quench our thirst we must stifle our smelling, and shut our nostrils when we opened our mouths'.

In the hottest of weathers each man's water ration was only a quart per day. So whilst becalmed it was a blessing that a torrential downpour came to rejuvenate them. They had seen no rain for over two months, and drinking rainwater after weeks of the ship's rancid water was a joy: Ovington says it tasted better than the richest wine. The sailors could not wait for the tubs set on deck to fill, but eagerly caught rain in hats and bowls. The shower was not sufficient to replenish the ship's stores of water, so it still had to be rationed but it did leave everyone refreshed.

As they marvelled at the plentiful supply of fruits and wild deer ashore, water suddenly presented them with a new problem. A large, twisting, waterspout developed right in front of them:

> 'We espied very near us a mighty mass of water drawn up into the air from the surface of the ocean, in fashion of a large round pipe, encircled with a hoary mist or grey cloud… This spout which is a kind of aqueduct between the clouds and ocean, put us in a great fear of its ruinous descent upon us.'

The captain steered the *Benjamin* away from the waterspout and eventually it collapsed, with Ovington noting that no ship could possibly have withstood the weight of water which fell when it did so. He describes two methods recommended for withstanding waterspout damage if a ship is drawn into one: the first was to read a passage from St John's gospel as a kind of charm, the other was to fire a cannon to break up the column of water. Even Ovington thought the first of these an unlikely cure, but with obvious amazement at what he had seen, he notes that, 'the works of the Almighty are inscrutable'.

## Dangers Await

The *Benjamin* docked at Malemba in the Kingdom of Kakongo, part of present-day Angola, and after meeting some eminent locals, they managed to replenish the ship's provisions before sailing for the remote island of St Helena. This passage took nearly a month, but once there the heat was mercifully much reduced. While anchored, a slave ship arrived carrying black natives from Madagascar to New York. The ship's commander warned that three pirate ships were docked at the other end of the island, which was often used as a pirate base.

Setting sail shortly thereafter, and avoiding the pirates, the *Benjamin* made the Cape of Good Hope at the southern end of Africa in three weeks, yet in rounding or 'doubling' the Cape, they ran into a fearsome storm. Captain

Browne, 'a stout and expert mariner', had doubled the Cape nine times in his career and even he confessed that he had not seen a storm of such ferocity. The wind was violent, the seas ran to great heights, and the thunder and lightning was 'frightful and amazing'. Ovington and his fellow passengers were battened down below decks, but as the noise of the storm grew louder the 'oaths and execrations' of the sailors grew louder still as if competing with the elements.

Eventually they made it through but were almost immediately presented with another crisis. In the early hours, Captain Browne took the *Benjamin* up Mozambique Channel, the stretch of water between Madagascar and mainland Africa.

> 'We were carried nearer this coast [Madagascar] than consistent either with our designs or safety, and would thereby have been driven directly upon a shelf of rocks that lay off from the shore, had not the watchful sailors upon the decks espied breakers [rolling waves] and, all amazed, cried out at the immediate hazard of our lives that we all were in. It was about four in the morning, and the faint glimmerings of the moon shed an imperfect light – just enough to give us a sight of our danger, and of avoiding it before we were upon it.'

The ship was saved from wrecking by sharp eyes, quick reactions and good fortune. Out of danger, the *Benjamin* sailed on to the island of Johanna, now known as Anjouan and part of the modern-day Union of Comoros at the northerly end of the Mozambique Channel. Here their ship was once more re-provisioned while Ovington explored the island and met its prince. The timing of their departure was fortunate once again, since shortly afterwards another East India Company ship, the *Herbert*, was attacked there by French warships and blown up.

## India at Last

The *Benjamin* continued north-eastwards, passed into the Arabian Sea, and was spared further dangers. Those on board realised India was near when snakes swam past them and locusts settled in the rigging, but the *Benjamin* was approaching Bombay (modern Mumbai) at the worst possible time:

'It was just the season of the monsoon when we fell upon the coast of India, which generally is extremely dangerous because they break out for the most part in such thunder and rains and impetuous winds that if the ships are not laid up and in harbour before that time they incur the hazard of being lost.'

Sure enough, a storm whipped up and threatened to wreck the ship, but a lull after 24 hours allowed the *Benjamin* to anchor safely. It was now 29 May 1690: it had taken an incredible 13½ months to reach here from England.

Unfortunately, much to everyone's frustration after so long a voyage, the ship was now trapped at Bombay until the monsoon season ended. The earliest they could leave was September, and they did not wish to stay any later than was essential, as Ovington explains:

'At Bombay, September and October – those two months which immediately follow the rains – are very pernicious to the health of the Europeans; in which two moons more of them die than generally in all the year besides. For the excess of earthy vapours after the rains ferment the air and raise therein such a sultry heat that scarce any is able to withstand that feverish effect.'

Water enables malaria mosquitoes to breed, and encourages freer transmission of diseases such as typhoid and dysentery. And so, to great alarm, people on the *Benjamin* began to die. By mid–September 20 of the 24 passengers were dead, and 15 of the *Benjamin*'s crew had gone the same way. They knew they could not survive much longer and so were relieved to depart for Surat. Ovington – predictably, given his calling – blamed the moral corruption of the inhabitants of Bombay for the diseases that prevailed there.

After visiting the island of Elephanta, the *Benjamin* sailed for Surat but pirates once again threatened. Yet on closer inspection they were, as Ovington notes, a 'puny' force 'who finding us a ship of force durst not attempt upon us'.

At long last they reached Surat in October, some 18 months after leaving London. Everyone could go ashore, where they 'met with an agreeable reception and kind entertainment' from the East India

Company's employees. Ovington was to spend two-and-a-half years there as a clergyman – a place considerably different to his native Yorkshire. Quite apart from the recurring monsoons, it was often so hot that the ink dried in his pen before he could write with it, and he could hardly bear to go outside in the heat after 3 pm. Nonetheless he honoured his contract and was so well-appreciated as a minister that on his return to England in 1693 the East India Company doubled his wages.

*Chapter Four*

# Health Trip to Europe

## *(1754, Henry Fielding,* Queen of Portugal*)*

Henry Fielding was a writer, dramatist, magistrate and founder of London's first police force, the so-called 'Bow Street Runners'. He was a man of great talent, yet at the time of this voyage his health was in serious decline, despite being only 47 years of age. Gout made him lame and he also suffered from jaundice, emaciation, fluctuating appetite, breathlessness, fatigue and fluid accumulation (or 'dropsy'). All of these symptoms have many potential causes, but taken together they indicate serious chronic illness, perhaps cancer.

In his account, Fielding revealed that he was 'in the opinion of all men, dying of a complication of disorders'. A doctor had managed to drain off considerable quantities of fluid from his swollen abdomen which temporarily eased his discomfort and breathing problems, but he decided to move to a warmer climate in the hope of improving his condition. He chose Lisbon, the capital of Britain's long-term ally, Portugal, and thus the idea for the voyage was born.

## Preparing to Depart

The travelling party was to consist of six: Fielding, his wife Mary, his daughter Harriot [sic] with her friend Margaret, a maid called Isabella, and his footman, William. They made quick plans: 'It was not difficult to find a ship bound to a place with which we carry on so immense a trade. Accordingly, my brother [John] soon informed me of the excellent accommodations for passengers which were to be found on board a ship that was obliged to sail for Lisbon in three days'.

This vessel was the *Queen of Portugal*, under Captain Richard Veale. Unfortunately, having prepared to depart, the sailing was delayed twice.

Niggled by this inefficiency, Fielding invited the captain to dinner to finalise matters. Captain Veale advised Fielding to board the following Wednesday – 26 June 1754. The voyage was expected to last three weeks and cost Fielding £30.

On the appointed day, Fielding's party was rowed out to the ship at Rotherhithe, although getting into the small open boat was difficult for Fielding as he could barely move unaided. Once the boat was tethered to the ship, the sailors tied Fielding to a chair and hauled him up the ship's side like a piece of cargo. To his indignation, the watching sailors and boatmen ridiculed him:

> 'The total loss of limbs was apparent to all who saw me, and my face contained marks of a most diseased state, if not of death itself… In this condition, I ran the gauntlet (so I think I may justly call it) through rows of sailors and watermen, few of whom failed of paying their compliments to me by all manner of insults and jests on my misery.'

A sailor also derided the passengers on the *Mayflower* for being ill. Perhaps this illustrates that even 130 years later, passengers were still something of a novelty to most crews of commercial ships who dealt principally in cargo. The more delicate business of handling passengers was far less familiar.

Fielding's state of mind was not improved when told that the ship would not sail the next day, as planned, because it was a public holiday and the Custom House, where Captain Veale needed to clear his paperwork, would be closed. Nonetheless, Fielding was carried to the captain's cabin – the most commodious living space on board – which was to accommodate him during the voyage. However, unhappily, the meal he was served further upset him:

> 'A sirloin of beef was now placed upon the table, for which – though little better than carrion – as much was charged by the master of the little paltry alehouse who dressed it, as would have been demanded for all the elegance of the King's Arms or any other polite tavern or eating-house.'

Passengers were expected to provide their own food and the party had brought provisions with them, but food was very important to Fielding, who was used to eating well.

On Thursday, Captain Veale embarked and began remonstrating with Fielding's party because they kept complaining. Taken aback, Fielding realised that 'all this was meant as an apology to introduce another procrastination (being the fifth) of his weighing anchor; which was now postponed until Saturday'. This latest delay was because the captain had to await a late shipment. Once again, the passengers' needs were rated less important than the profitability of cargo.

Fielding discovered the captain was formerly a privateer, a role somewhere between a licensed pirate and the commander of a private warship. Privateers took advantage of war to plunder enemy shipping with the Crown's approval. This experience encouraged Captain Veale to sport a sword and a military-style cockade on his hat – neither of which were appropriate for a merchant ship's officer. Veale was 70 years old with 46 years' experience at sea and 'while he was deaf himself, had a voice capable of deafening others'.

Fielding worried that the delays might lead him to require medical attention at sea for his swollen abdomen. Surprisingly, the *Queen* had its own surgeon which probably reflected Veale's experience of privateering, where a surgeon was an essential crew member. Yet ships' surgeons at this time had limited medical experience and were not highly regarded. Sure enough, Fielding discovered their surgeon was also 'steward, cook, butler, and sailor'. So he summoned his friend, the surgeon John Hunter, who tapped off 'ten quarts of water' from the bloated Fielding.

## Cruising the Thames

Fielding's improvement at the hands of Mr Hunter was marred by Mrs Fielding's all-night toothache. Early on Sunday, with the ship due to sail, she resolved to have the tooth removed, so footman William was sent for a 'tooth-drawer'. But the *Queen of Portugal* departed before he could return and William had to chase the ship along the Thames before rejoining at Gravesend. Fielding blamed the ship's pilot for this because he refused to wait.

Despite this aggravation, Fielding enjoyed a pleasurable voyage down the Thames on a bright morning. They passed hundreds of ships – the Thames being then the busiest waterway in Britain – yachts, colliers, coasters, transport vessels and the magnificent ships of the East India Company. He admired this portion of the nation's mercantile fleet with pride: 'the whole forms a most pleasing object to the eye, as well as highly warming to the heart of an Englishman'. Yet, beyond the 'delightful' Royal Naval Hospital at Greenwich, Fielding was surprised at the few houses on the riverbank until they reached Gravesend at the mouth of the Thames.

Once anchored, Fielding sent for a surgeon to attend to Mary's toothache. The captain meanwhile provisioned the ship with fresh stores, particularly beans and peas, to accompany the salt meat he already had on board.

This wasn't to be the end of Sunday's events however. The family sat down for Sunday lunch, pleased to be on their way and grateful for Mrs Fielding's freedom from pain. Fielding recounts what happens next:

'On a sudden the window on one side was beat into the room with a crash, as if a twenty-pounder [cannonball] had been discharged among us. We were all alarmed at the suddenness of the accident for which, however, we were soon able to account: for the sash, which was shivered all to pieces, was pursued into the middle of the cabin by the bowsprit of a little ship called a cod-smack, the master of which made us amends for running (carelessly at best) against us in the sea-way. That is to say, by damning us all to hell, and uttering several pious wishes that it had done us much more mischief.'

Perhaps the next day would bring an end to Fielding's harassments? Sadly, no. For as husband and wife sat together in the afternoon 'two ruffians' burst into their cabin unannounced. And to make matters worse, one of them even failed to remove his hat in front of Mrs Fielding. After a lecture on manners from Fielding, the men apologised and only then were given the opportunity to reveal themselves as customs officers, sent to check that the proper duty had been paid on the cargo and the necessary paperwork completed.

Eventually, at six o'clock with a favourable wind and tide the *Queen* weighed anchor and sailed down to the Nore, the sandbank at the easternmost end of the Thames estuary. Here the river meets the North Sea and the ship turned southward towards the English Channel.

## The Channel Coast

On Tuesday, 2 July, the *Queen of Portugal* sailed down the Kent coast and anchored on the Downs, a stretch of the North Sea bordered to westward by the coast near Deal, and to the east by the treacherous Goodwin Sands. It is a roadstead that has been used by ships for centuries as the water is deep, and it also offers some protection from bad weather.

Poor Mrs Fielding was again suffering from toothache. A surgeon from Deal unsuccessfully attempted to remove the culprit, and she retired early to bed. With daughter Harriot and her friend both seasick, Fielding sought company elsewhere but the only other passengers were not to his liking: 'a rude schoolboy of fourteen years old, and an illiterate Portuguese friar who understands no language but his own'. Desperate for conversation, Fielding summoned the captain but his deafness proved exasperating – Fielding had to shout loudly – so both men sat drinking punch until they fell asleep.

The next morning, detained by a contrary wind, Fielding sent his footman ashore to replenish their provisions. Despite the fresh food, Harriot and Margaret were still too seasick to eat, and Mary preferred simply to sleep, so after a lonely roast mutton meal Fielding later shared the evening with the captain as before.

On Friday, Fielding spied a warship and sent a letter to her captain asking if its longboat might row the ladies to Dover, seven miles away, for their entertainment. To back up this preposterous request, he mentioned the wife of Lord Anson, First Lord of the Admiralty, a woman he had never even met. The warship's captain, unimpressed, returned a simple verbal 'no' to Fielding's long letter – an impoliteness that outraged the easily-outraged Fielding, and in his journal he railed against the 'petty tyrants' called captains who seemed to lack any civility.

Captain Veale attempted to weigh anchor despite not having a fair wind, but suffered a second collision for his trouble: a small sloop ran foul of them and lost its bowsprit. In the afternoon, the crew fished from the ship to supplement their rations and caught a great number of whiting.

At last, early one morning, the wind changed and the *Queen of Portugal* set sail. The wind was feeble but with the tide in their favour they cruised past the cliffs of Dover and by Tuesday morning were in sight of the Isle of

Wight. Here a gale blew up and the captain was forced to take refuge at Ryde on the mainland side of the island where, once the storm abated, they again became trapped by an unfavourable wind. Whilst there, a kitten, one of four cats on the ship, fell overboard but the boatswain stripped off and dived in to save it.

## Coast Bound

By the weekend, it was clear that the contrary wind would persist for days and the Fieldings elected to decamp to Ryde until the wind changed. Fielding was hoisted into a small boat and manhandled ashore to his lodgings. Predictably, he was soon quarrelling with his landlady, Mrs Francis, about almost everything. It is clear that having recently occupied a post of authority, Fielding expected complete deference and obedience from anyone he regarded as his social inferior.

They stayed ten days with Mrs Francis, the 'fury', until the captain arrived to tell them the wind was about to blow favourably. Veale was anxious to depart without delay – especially as moving Fielding was a cumbersome business – and one can imagine his exasperation at being told his passengers would come after completing breakfast. The Fieldings delayed even further by hunting for a lost tea chest and then, unsurprisingly, arguing with the landlady over the bill. Eventually, all was prepared and they re-embarked.

Unfortunately, Captain Veale was quite wrong about the wind and it did not alter course as he had predicted. They were stuck where they were before. It was now almost a month since the ship had left London, yet the passengers were still in England.

The next day at Spithead, the stretch of the Solent between Ryde and Portsmouth, the captain entertained his nephew, a lieutenant in the army recently returned from the Mediterranean. True to form, Fielding took an instant dislike to this boisterous officer, but fortunately he was soon saved further exposure when the wind changed direction. The lieutenant was quickly dumped ashore and the *Queen* set sail. The brisk wind carried them along the coast to Portland in Dorset, but having reached there, the wind suddenly stood against them once more.

The weather deteriorated into a storm, forcing the *Queen* landwards for protection. The women started to be seasick again and so Fielding was left alone in his cabin all day. In the evening, he was obliged to socialise with the captain and soon deduced that he was lost: the next morning he witnessed Veale's surprise when the ship's carpenter announced that they were now lying off Torbay in Devon.

Turning his attention to food once more, Fielding quickly obtained clotted cream, fresh butter and bread from the shore for breakfast. But the good humour was again brief; this time Fielding argued with a local boatman over his fare to row William ashore for cider.

While still off the coast of Devon, local fishermen came out to sell them fish. Fielding was delighted with the quality and cheapness of the fish and his party enjoyed a fine lunch. Unfortunately, once again Fielding's happiness was short-lived, for while finishing their meal the captain's steward walked into their cabin to pack down some beer into bottles, without so much as a by-your-leave. Incensed at the interruption, Fielding sent the steward away, feeling that having paid to use the captain's cabin as their own, they deserved privacy. But the captain was unable to tolerate Fielding's countermanding his orders and vented a voyage-full of frustration at him:

> '"Your cabin!" repeated he many times. "No, damn me! 'Tis my cabin. Your cabin! Damn me! I have brought my hogs to a fair market. I suppose indeed you think it your cabin, and your ship, by your commanding in it; but I will command in it, damn me! I will show the world I am the commander, and nobody but I! Did you think I sold you the command of my ship for that pitiful thirty pounds? I wish I had not seen you nor your thirty pounds aboard of her".'

Fielding continues:

> 'The captain poured forth such a torrent of abuse that I very hastily and very foolishly resolved to quit the ship. I gave immediate orders to summon a hoy [coastal vessel] to carry me that evening to Dartmouth, without considering any consequence... I likewise threatened the

captain with that which, he afterwards said, he feared more than any rock or quicksand [ie legal action].'

It is the biggest argument in an account full of arguments. Yet at the prospect of losing his passengers' fares and of being sued, the poor old captain 'tumbled on his knees and, a little too abjectly, implored mercy'. Fielding magnanimously forgave him, but privately assured his readers that he only did so because it was convenient to do it.

Over the next couple of days Fielding began to worry again about his fluid retention and called on board a local surgeon who tapped off sufficient to relieve his discomfort. Meanwhile the ladies took a walk on shore to relieve the monotony. The poor captain, however, began to believe their lack of wind for days on end was due to witchcraft – the sorceress being none other than the vicious Mrs Francis, the landlady from Ryde!

However, a change soon came. On Saturday, 29 July, after five interminable days, a favourable wind set the ship on its way westwards. The weather was so pleasant that the Fielding party sat on deck to catch the sun. Fielding marvelled that they had more than 30 other ships around them as they passed Dartmouth, which had all been in the same situation, waiting for the right wind.

## Journey to Lisbon

On Sunday they sighted Plymouth and then the Lizard, the most southerly point of Cornwall. Being the Lord's day, the captain summoned all hands to prayers 'which were read by a common sailor upon deck with more devout force and address than they are commonly read by a country curate'. With the swell of the Atlantic moving the ship, the women returned to their seasickness, leaving Fielding again alone in his cabin.

The *Queen* then entered the Bay of Biscay where they were temporarily becalmed. The crew hung a piece of salt beef over the side to freshen it, but a shark swallowed it. Undeterred, they launched a second piece of beef over the side, this time hiding a large hook. When the culprit took the bait, the crew hauled in the shark and retrieved both pieces of beef for the pot and cooked the shark as well.

The ship could only make intermittent progress across the Bay, the wind picking up, only to desert them again. There was even a short gale where Fielding could see the angry sea from his cabin:

'It rose mountains high, and lifted our poor ship up and down, backwards and forwards, with so violent an emotion, that there was scarce a man in the ship better able to stand than myself. Every utensil in our cabin rolled up and down, as we should have rolled ourselves, had not our chairs been fast lashed to the floor. In this situation, with our tables likewise fastened by ropes, the captain and myself took our meal with some difficulty, and swallowed a little of our broth, for we spilt much the greater part.'

By the evening on Thursday, a north-westerly wind was bowling the ship along at nearly ten knots as they approached Cape Finisterre. Yet before dusk they were again becalmed, although they did enjoy a magnificent sunset.

Friday began with a contrary SSE wind, which would not allow them to make for Lisbon. The captain beat out to sea, but the passengers were now out of fresh provisions: 'Even our bread was come to an end, and nothing but sea biscuit remained, which I could not chew. So that now, for the first time in my life, I saw what it was to want a bit of bread'.

Saturday saw an improvement in the wind, and on Sunday, after prayers, a gentle yet favourable wind persisted. But the swell set the ship rolling, and this time even Fielding experienced seasickness with 'bowels almost twisted out of my belly'. The ship continued on apace, however, cruising down the coast of Portugal towards their final destination. On Tuesday they reached the mouth of the river Tagus, which allows entrance from the sea to the port of Lisbon. Here the *Queen of Portugal* moored, waiting for the tide to turn in their favour, and to pick up a pilot to navigate them further.

At noon, a pilot navigated them into the Tagus and they cruised to within three miles of Lisbon where a shore gun indicated they must go no further without authorisation. The ship received a magistrate of health who inspected the ship for signs of infectious disease: he insisted that everyone be drawn up on deck for inspection, including the unfortunate Fielding who was hauled up with the rest. Next, customs officers came on board to ensure dues were paid, and to inspect the *Queen* for tobacco, an illegal import. These officials executed their duty 'with great insolence', rifling through everyone's personal possessions, but the knowing sailors had already advised their passengers to take care of their belongings as these men often stole valuables on the pretext of conducting a thorough search.

At midnight, the vessel was allowed to proceed to Lisbon and cast anchor 'in a calm and a moonshiny night' which was so pleasant that the ladies stayed on deck for three hours to enjoy it.

Late morning the next day, Fielding sent William ashore to find the party a place to eat and to secure a carriage. He returned three hours later to say that the port's chief officer, or provedore, had to issue a permit to allow foreign passengers to disembark. The provedore was currently on a siesta and they would have to wait. Eventually, the permit was issued and Fielding was carried ashore at 7 pm. He remarked, with admirable restraint, that 'I never yet saw or heard of a place where a traveller had so much trouble given him at his landing as here'.

Fielding had reached his final destination on 9 August, some 44 days after setting out and more than double the expected journey time of 21 days. Yet after all they had been through, Fielding, true to form, took an immediate dislike to Lisbon as he was wheeled through it in his chaise, describing it as 'the nastiest city in the world'! Unfortunately he was to die there not long after his arrival.

*Chapter Five*

# Visiting the Caribbean

## *(1774, Janet Schaw*, Jamaica Packet*)*

At 9 o'clock in the evening on 25 October 1774, Janet Schaw and her entourage boarded the small 80-ton brig *Jamaica Packet* at Burntisland in Fife. The party included her brother, Alexander and his Indian servant, Robert, her own maid or 'abigail', Mary Miller, and the three children of a family friend – Fanny, Jack and Billy Rutherford. The children had been sent to Scotland to be educated but were now returning to North Carolina where Janet was to be reunited with another brother, and Alexander was travelling to the Caribbean as a customs officer.

The three ladies were berthed together, and in her journal Miss Schaw describes their accommodation as small and disagreeable, mainly because it was so dirty: 'nothing can be less cleanly than our cabin, unless it be its commander'.

'Our bed chamber, which is dignified with the title of State Room, is about five foot wide and six long; on one side is a bed fitted up for Miss Rutherford and on the opposite side one for me. Poor Fanny's is so very narrow, that she is forced to be tied in, or as the sea term is lashed in, to prevent her falling over. On the floor below us lies our abigail, Mrs Mary, now Mrs Miller. As she has the breadth of both our beds and excellent bedding, I think she has got a most enviable berth, but this is far from her opinion.'

There was a different arrangement for the male passengers. Alexander slept in a cot swinging from the roof of his cabin, and the two boys shared a bed on the floor below him.

They had all just got to bed when the party was roused by the order to weigh anchor: 'Everybody that was able, got up to see this first grand operation…

all hands were on deck. Hurry, bustle, noise, and confusion raged through our wooden kingdom, yet it was surprising how soon everything was reduced to order. In little more than a quarter of an hour, all was over'.

## A Few Surprises

Going to bed was not straightforward because there was so little space: the ladies had to prepare for bed one by one. And once at sea, shipboard noises meant no guarantee of rest: the sound of the crew's feet on the planking above, the captain talking and barking orders, the calls for changes of watch, and the cockerel in the hen coop above their heads. They were also disturbed by poor Fanny's seasickness. Alexander tried giving her a few drops of salt water to settle her stomach, but his servant Robert provided the best solution – chicken broth.

The captain of the *Jamaica Packet*, Thomas Smith, had planned to sail to Dover, along the English Channel and then into the Atlantic. However, shortly after sailing, the wind shifted and blew 'full in our teeth' so that the original route became impossible. He thus decided to head north and to round the top of Scotland instead. As Miss Schaw points out, this would be a far less comfortable route:

'It is hardly possible to imagine a more disagreeable passage at this season of the year than this must be. The many islands, shelves and rocks, render it very dangerous, which, with the addition of a rough sea, sudden squalls, and the coldest climate in Britain, gives as uncomfortable a prospect as one would wish.'

Soon all Miss Schaw's party were seasick, but Alexander and Fanny were badly affected. Their misery was not helped by the bitter cold weather, the constant rain, and being 'jaulted to death by the motion of the ship in these rough seas'. The movement of the ship was so bad that Miss Schaw and Fanny could not keep their footing and stayed in their cabin. They began to worry about the health of the threadbare crew who were constantly wet and frozen, and Miss Schaw notes that the rascally owner, George Parker, had equipped the ship with less than half the seamen he had promised them.

A mere eight men worked the ship; this left little spare capacity in case of illness.

The weather improved on their third day, and Alexander encouraged his sister to go on deck for fresh air. George Parker had charged them a surprisingly high fee for their passage, but justified it by assuring them they would be the only passengers on board so would have the comfort of plenty of space:

> 'We now ascended the companion or cabin stairs when, judge of my surprise, I saw the deck covered with people of all ages, from three weeks old to three score: men, women, children and suckling infants. For some time I was unable to credit my senses, it appeared a scene raised by the power of magic to bring such a crowd together in the middle of the sea, when I believed there was not a soul aboard but the ship's crew and our own family'.

These were steerage passengers accommodated in crude and cramped conditions below decks to the stern of the ship. George Parker had lied to them again. Even the captain described him as a villain and a scoundrel, although Miss Schaw was liable to believe they were as bad as one another.

The steerage passengers were Scottish emigrants to America, and Miss Schaw says that they smelled very much – not helped of course by their seasickness – and she was afraid they might infect her with something. At this time certain diseases were believed to be transmitted as a kind of vapour, and so bad odours were credited as indicating disease 'in the air'.

Surprisingly, despite the cold, cramped conditions and shipboard noises, Miss Schaw rapidly adapted to life at sea and learned to sleep soundly. Eating was an experience initially tempered by their continued seasickness. At breakfast time, none of them found they could tolerate much, but eggs seemed to go down well. Unfortunately, they trusted the crooked George Parker to arrange supplies of bread, which he did not, and the ship's biscuit he had provided was described by Miss Schaw as fit only for pigs.

One breakfast time while they attempted to keep their food down, the unpleasantly odorous captain suddenly arrived and ruined everything: 'The nasty captain... set all our stomachs topsy-turvy by the smell. My brother flew to the deck, Miss Rutherford to her state room, I applied to my smelling bottle'.

Going on deck to watch the Scottish islands slip by in the cold wind, Miss Schaw observed the sorrowful steerage passengers who had been evicted from the very shores that now sped by. She became acquainted with Mr and Mrs Lawson, who had three children on board. This family had worked their land for many generations and had been well-off, but their farm was rented and the landlord, eager to secure the land for himself, raised the rent to unaffordable levels, forcing them out of their home. The Lawsons were obliged to emigrate as they had nowhere else to go. Other emigrants shared similar stories about what has become known as the Highland Clearances: wealthy landowners maximising their incomes by ousting tenant farmers. To make matters worse, the malignant ship owner, George Parker, aware of their desperation to leave, had charged the emigrants double the normal fare.

## The Storm

Shortly afterwards, as Miss Schaw sat reading by a small stove, the winds began to blow hard about the ship. Suddenly, she heard a rumbling sound behind her: 'What was my surprise, when the cabin-door burst open and I was overwhelmed with an immense wave, which broke my chair from its moorings, floated everything in the cabin, and I found myself swimming amongst joint-stools, chests, tables and all the various furniture of our parlour'.

Fanny had now recovered from her seasickness but Alexander was still badly affected. Miss Schaw tended him as best she could but the increasingly heavy weather didn't help. As it deteriorated into a gale, the captain sent the ship's carpenter to put up the shutters (or 'dead lights') outside their cabin windows to stop water coming in, but this also cut out the daylight.

In the event, the gale lasted ten or twelve days and Miss Schaw gave up writing her journal during this time. The captain seemed happy initially as the ship was making a good ten knots but the storm rapidly worsened. Recalling her experiences in her journal afterwards, she describes their dark cabin with its single candle as being like a tomb, and that the sea became alarming to behold:

'The sea was now running mountain high, and the waves so outrageous, that they came aboard like a deluge; and rushing from side to side of the vessel, generally made their way into the cabin, and from thence into the stateroom, which was often so full of water as almost to reach us in our beds. Poor Mary had now real cause to complain, as she was actually very near drowned while asleep, and could no longer lie in the state room but was forced to peg in with the boys.'

The sailors stayed on deck, soaking, for hours on end, and at midnight on the fourth night the dreadful call of 'all hands' was given. This meant an emergency where every crew member was obliged to help work the ship to ensure its survival. Even the male passengers helped. Water poured below decks soaking Miss Schaw and Fanny in their beds. The noise was incredible. The storm ripped away the entire kitchen and the hen–coop from the main deck, together with all the provisions they contained; sails were torn to shreds and the ship no longer responded to the helm. They were at the mercy of the elements. Finally the ship could take no more and the fore mainmast split from top to bottom.

By next morning, the storm had lessened but it continued for several more days. During this time, Miss Schaw's party survived on a large ham that Robert had prepared when he saw the storm approaching. No fires could be lit for cooking during the storm as they were either dowsed by the incoming seawater or risked being upturned and setting the ship alight. So their meals for ten days or so consisted of cold ham, together with wine and biscuits.

However, Miss Schaw's situation was better than that endured by the steerage passengers who had been battened down into the crowded airless space below decks:

'For many days together, they could not lie down, but sat supporting their little ones in their arms, who must otherwise have been drowned. No victuals [meals] could be dressed, nor fire got on, so that all they had to subsist on, was some raw potatoes, and a very small proportion of mouldy brisket. In this condition they remained for nine days, with scarcely any interval, (Good heavens! Poor creatures) without light, meat or air, with the immediate prospect of death before them.'

One poor woman became so frightened that she miscarried during the gale. Her husband managed to break open the hatches and take her on deck, fearing she was dead, and the fresh air helped to revive her.

The most alarming moment of the whole storm came when the *Jamaica Packet* suddenly 'broached to' without warning. The ship was brought abruptly broadside-on to the wind and the waves, so that the full force of the elements came suddenly to bear on only one side and overturned the whole ship leaving its masts lying in the water. Miss Schaw vividly describes the effects from her perspective:

> 'The ship gave such a sudden and violent heel over, as broke everything from their moorings, and in a moment the great sea-chests, the boys' bed, my brother's cot, Miss Rutherford's harpsichord, with tables, chairs, joint-stools, pewter plates etc, etc., together with Fanny, Jack and myself, were tumbling heels over head to the side the vessel had laid down on. It is impossible to describe the horror of our situation. The candle was instantly extinguished, and all this going on in the dark, without the least idea of what produced it, or what was to be its end. The captain sprung on deck the moment he felt the first motion, for he knew well enough its consequence. To complete the horror of the scene, the sea poured in on us, over my brother's head, who held fast the ladder though almost drowned, while we were floated by a perfect deluge.'

Fortunately, the ship's masts were by now so damaged that they were snapped off by this unexpected motion of the vessel, and the instant decrease in 'top-weight' allowed the *Jamaica Packet* to roll back upright once more. They were very fortunate indeed; the majority of ships in this situation foundered.

The ship had become a ruinous mess. In her cabin, Miss Schaw had a cut on her forehead and found herself covered in molasses after a barrel had spilled its contents all over her. None of her party was seriously injured, although the last of the live poultry they had brought on board, a poor duck, was 'squeezed as flat as a pancake'.

## Aftermath

Eventually they were able to light a fire, begin clearing up and take stock. Although they were only about halfway to their destination, most of their food had been lost in the storm. They had paid handsomely to use the ship's provisions when their own ran out, and George Parker, the owner, had given Miss Schaw a 'splendid list' of the fare available. Yet the villainous Parker had deceived them once again – everything that Miss Schaw asked for from his list 'had been unfortunately forgot'. When she demanded to know what food was available, she was horrified to learn there was only salt beef, salt pork, oatmeal, herrings and potatoes.

They managed to find a little of their own butter, onions, cheese and eggs that had survived the storm, and somehow their servants, Mary and Robert, managed to make them something wonderful every day.

'For example, lobscouse is one of the most savoury dishes I ever ate. It is composed of salt beef hung by a string over the side of the ship, till rendered tolerably fresh, then cut in nice little pieces, and with potatoes, onions and pepper, is stewed for some time, with the addition of a proportion of water. This is my favourite dish; but scratch-platter, chowder, stir-about, and some others have all their own merit.'

Miss Schaw felt she could not complain when she realised how little the steerage passengers ate. They were given a pound of meat, two pounds of oatmeal and a few very mouldy ship biscuits. This had to last each adult a whole *week*. Fortunately they had brought some potatoes with them to eke out their shipboard rations.

When the steerage passengers were allowed out of their confinement, new woes awaited them. The adverse conditions meant that their travel chests had been underwater for over two weeks. When they were retrieved, the seawater had found its way in and ruined their possessions. Many of the women broke down at this. Misfortune seemed to heap upon misfortune.

Meanwhile the *Jamaica Packet* had been blown severely off course and was a mess. Captain Smith set about picking through the jumble on deck to see what was worth saving, and the crew began preparing jury masts to replace those that had been lost. These were short, temporary replacements made from whatever lengthy timbers could be found on board, such as spars. They were designed to hold enough sail to keep the ship moving. Fortunately, ships generally carried a supply of spare timber for repairs, and a sufficient number of spare sails to replace those lost in storms.

## Fair and Foul and Fair Again

The weather kept fair, so Miss Schaw's party, now free from seasickness, could pass their time on board more pleasurably. They spent many days on deck enjoying the sunshine. Mary, Miss Schaw's often crotchety servant, became enamoured of a sailor named Davy, and his affections sweetened her ill humour. But love turned to bitterness when Mary discovered he was paying attention to another woman at the same time.

Miss Schaw enjoyed watching the sharks, fish and turtles over the side of the ship in the warm weather. There was music too: Alexander played his flute to accompany Fanny on the harpsichord, and some of the steerage passengers sang. Despite all this pleasantry, Alexander began to suspect that the captain was lost, which disconcerted the rest of the party. Miss Schaw made a bet with the captain that they were less than 100 miles from land; he did not agree and took up the wager readily. Yet within 24 hours Miss Schaw was proved correct, for the next day they sighted the Azores. They gleefully prepared a list of all the provisions they required but, unfortunately, the 'brute of a captain' repeatedly refused to allow them on shore to replenish their supplies.

Captain Smith was afraid that his ship would be captured by Barbary pirates 'with which these seas are terribly infested'. These frightening raiders were very different to the Dunkirkers encountered by Thomas Dallam in 1599 (Chapter 1). The Barbary pirates or 'corsairs' were based in North Africa – principally Algiers, Tunis and Tripoli – and attacked merchant shipping to seize the vessel and the cargo as prizes, and to take the people on board as slaves. Britain had a treaty with the Barbary states, paying them not to attack its ships, and the Admiralty issued 'passes' to British vessels so they could go unmolested. Captain Smith, having originally intended to pursue a route well away from the pirates' usual haunts, had no pass. So if accosted by a corsair, they were in grave danger – the crew especially, since they were bound to be enslaved – but passengers were often released to the British consul once back in north Africa. In 1661, the diarist Samuel Pepys had written of his meeting some ex-slaves:

'went to the Fleece Tavern to drink; and there we spent till four o'clock, telling stories of Algiers, and the manner of the life of slaves there! And truly Captain Mootham and Mr Dawes (who have been both slaves there) did make me fully acquainted with their condition there: as, how they eat nothing but bread and water... How they are beat upon the soles of their feet and bellies at the liberty of their padron.'

And as if to confirm Smith's fears a strange ship appeared: '"Oh God!" cried the captain as he entered the cabin, "we are undone..."', but Alexander Schaw kept a cool head. He ordered his family to dress in their best apparel so that the corsairs might think them more fit for ransom than selling as slaves. While Miss Schaw and the party were in the middle of this quick change act, the strange ship suddenly veered off and was never seen again. They were safe.

Once they left the Azores, another 'terrible tempest' assaulted them, which meant that Miss Schaw could not keep her diary for five days. It resembled their previous storm 'with the addition of the most terrible thunder and lightning that ever were seen'. All their previous repairs were destroyed so the crew had to start again: 'We have not a stick standing nor a rag of sail to put up, and we lie tumbling amongst the waves. All hands are employed in making sails: our smiths and carpenter busy patching our bits of timber, so as to make something like masts'.

While in the midst of these desperate repairs they encountered a Royal Navy warship, the *Boyne*, but Miss Schaw bitterly records in her diary that they refused to offer any assistance, not even some spare timber.

The sailors sat down *en masse* with needle and thread and began repairing the tatters of sail that remained. Miss Schaw was impressed by their industry and the neatness of their work. Mended sails were soon in place on their battered stumpy masts, and they managed to catch a fair wind for the Caribbean.

## Entertainments

As they headed southwest, the passengers could enjoy time on deck in the warm sunshine. The crew rigged an awning so Miss Schaw could sit under it and write without getting too hot. The improving climate heralded other changes which helped to distract the passengers from their enforced meagre diet – bluer water, fiery sunsets and new constellations at night. There was new wildlife too, such as dolphins, porpoises and tropical birds. A small whale accompanied the ship for a while and the passengers amused themselves by throwing him food scraps to eat. These, and other diversions, were a welcome relief:

> 'The effect of this fine weather appears in every creature, even our emigrants seem in a great measure to have forgot their sufferings, and hope gives a gleam of pleasure even to the heartbroken features of Mrs Lawson, and if we had anything to eat, I really think our present situation is most delightful. We play at cards and backgammon on deck; the sailors dance hornpipes and jigs from morning to night; every lass has her lad.'

As Mary, Miss Schaw's servant, had discovered earlier in the voyage, the amorous escapades of men and women crammed together on a ship for several weeks can provoke incidents. The ship's cooper jumped into bed with one of the emigrant's wives but, finding himself rebuffed, claimed he had been thrown there by the motion of the ship!

As the temperatures soared, Miss Schaw's party abandoned their usual daytime clothing for light muslin, and at night slept under a single sheet. The steerage passengers slept on deck at night. Understandably, the heat increased the desire to bathe and the Schaw party now washed every morning. A large cask of water was prepared for them on deck and the decks cleared so that the ladies might not be seen in their scanty bathing suits and could wash unobserved.

The heat intensified near the Tropic of Cancer, and the passengers prepared for the ceremony of Crossing the Tropic. This has many similarities to that performed by ships crossing the equator (one version of which is described by Maria Graham in Chapter 6).

'We have been made to expect a visit from old Tropicus and his ancient dame. He is a wizard and she a witch who inhabit an invisible Island in these seas, and have a privilege of raising contributions from every ship that passes their dominions… Tropicus is performed by an old rough dog of a tar, who needs very little alteration to become a Caliban in mind and body, but his wife is played by a very handsome fellow, who is completely transformed. Everybody is below waiting, in trembling expectation …'

Tropicus demanded to know what strangers were on board who had not come this way before. The crew identified them and led them up on deck one at a time, blindfolded. Tropicus then asked them some questions, and the passengers were told that if they spoke the honest truth, then he shaved them, took a small gratuity for his trouble, gave them his benediction and let them pass. But if they disguised or concealed the truth, which he was supposed perfectly to know, then he tumbled them into the sea, where they perished.

The crew had rigged up a boat filled with water behind the blindfolded passengers, so that they might be tipped into it during the interrogation. Needless to say, they shrieked as they went in, fearing they had been thrown over the side of the ship. After they had had their fun with the passengers, custom dictated that the crew were allowed to hold mastery over their officers, and they chased them around the decks drenching them with buckets of water.

This had all been in good spirits but the captain began demanding that every passenger pay five shillings or they would be thrown into the sea from the top of the mainmast. The poor emigrants were distraught. They had no money, and raced to find possessions that the captain might take instead. Furious, Alexander Schaw turned on the captain, who maintained it was only to ensure the crew had some drinking money, so Alexander paid them all a suitable donation on behalf of everyone on board.

Notwithstanding this incident, the captain shortly produced a secret stash of beer. In the blazing heat, he charged the thirsty passengers two shillings a bottle, which extortionate price the Schaw party were happy to pay.

**Land Ho!**

Not long afterwards, Miss Schaw was the first passenger to sight land:

> '"Is not that land?" said I to the man at the helm.
>
> "Yes," said he, squirting out his quid of tobacco with great composure, "as soon as the mate will come up, I will show it to him".
>
> I did not wait [for] that ceremony, but turning round to the cabin, exclaimed as loud as I was able: "Land, land!" Everybody run up, such a whistling of joy, and such a shaking of hands. There was no doubt it was Antigua.'

On nearing the island, the crew sounded the depth of the water with a lead and line; as it became shallower it changed colour to a light blue and then to green. A pilot came aboard to guide the *Jamaica Packet* round the rocks, and Miss Schaw saw her first Caribbean plantations from the deck of the ship.

They dropped anchor about a mile from the town of St John's, and Miss Schaw's brother took a boat ashore to arrange their lodgings. This was the end of their Atlantic crossing which had taken seven weeks.

*Chapter Six*

# Trading Interests in South America

## *(1821, Maria Graham, Doris)*

Any account of British passenger experiences at sea naturally focuses on the role of what we now call the merchant navy in transporting them. However, from time to time the Royal Navy also had a role in carrying civilian passengers, often ferrying VIPs such as ambassadors. The navy's firepower helped ensure the safety of these individuals, but a military escort also reinforced the official nature of the passenger's business. Rival European powers or pirates might attack a merchant ship, but would think twice about tackling a warship.

In 1821, it was decided to send an armed ship to South America. Britain had trading interests in Chile, which had recently declared independence from Spain; and in Brazil which sought independence from Portugal. At this time of uncertainty, Britain needed to support its local merchants and make clear that it would protect its commerce by military means if necessary.

The ship chosen was the *Doris*, a 42-gun frigate with a complement of 240 under the command of Captain Thomas Graham. He took with him his well-travelled wife Maria as a passenger, together with her maid, and fortunately Mrs Graham kept a journal of her experiences.

## Outward Bound

HMS *Doris* left Portsmouth on 31 July 1821, and quickly made Ushant, an island that effectively marks the south-western end of the English Channel, but a heavy gale forced the ship back to Falmouth before it could enter the Bay of Biscay.

In the event it wasn't until 11 August that the *Doris* set sail once more. Three days out, following the voyage's resumption, the captain ordered all hands to witness the punishment of a crewman. Able seaman John Hood was given 30 lashes for drunkenness and 'pissing on the quarterdeck'. No doubt Mrs Graham would have stayed in her cabin for this; but despite his wife's presence on board, Captain Graham had to enforce discipline by the strict naval standards of the day. This was not the merchant navy, it was a military vessel. Drunkenness on board ship could never be tolerated – it was potentially a danger to everyone on board – and urinating on the deck was both indecent and disrespectful.

By 18 August the ship had anchored at Funchal on Madeira just in time to witness a beautiful sunset. This wasn't Mrs Graham's first visit and she accompanied some of the young officers ashore who had never travelled abroad before, helping them to explore the island. Together, they admired the unfamiliar flora, fauna, history and scenery.

The *Doris* stayed for four days, departing on 23 August. At night, Mrs Graham enjoyed listening to the songs that the sailors sang to while away the hours:

'I sat a long time on the deck, listening to the sea songs with which the crew beguile the evening watch. Though the humorous songs were applauded sufficiently, yet the plaintive and the pathetic seemed the favourites: and the chorus to the Death of [General] Wolfe was swelled by many voices.'

Since they usually worked in an all-male environment, sailors' songs could be rather bawdy, so no doubt these songs were either carefully selected or toned down by the crew to avoid offending the captain's wife.

On 25 August, the *Doris* reached Tenerife, a lofty blue peak poking through the clouds that veiled the island. The ship anchored in deep water but the Atlantic swell caused a constant lifting up and down of the vessel which Mrs Graham found unsettling. She went ashore with the first lieutenant, Mr Dance, who was entrusted to look after the captain's wife while his commanding officer was distracted by his official duties in port. Once again, Mrs Graham set about exploring on her own initiative. Returning to the ship at sunset proved awkward because of the swell which made it difficult to bring the ship's boat safely alongside the frigate. Mrs Graham and her maid were probably hoisted aboard via a boatswain's chair, a seat that was hauled up to the ship's deck via ropes. The rest of the boat's occupants, being crew members, were expected to scramble up the ship's side.

The next day, some of the local dignitaries she had met the day before were rowed out to the ship and were entertained on board, yet the swell made all but one of them very seasick.

Leaving the Canary Islands three days later, the *Doris* headed south and Mrs Graham delighted to watch out for wildlife. She saw large numbers of flying fish, 'whole fleets' of jellyfish, and a beautiful purple sea snail. Although over 400 miles from land, she was amazed that a fine yellow locust and a swallow flew on board and stopped with them to rest.

One of Mrs Graham's roles on board was to lend a hand in the teaching of young crew members. Midshipmen always received an education under the auspice of the captain, to prepare them to become commissioned officers, but Captain Graham had also established a school for the ship's boys who aspired to become seamen. This task was headed by Mr Hyslop, a schoolmaster appointed by Captain Graham: 'He is most anxious to make them fit to be officers and seamen in their profession, and good men and gentlemen both at sea and on shore'. The idea was to impose on these young men a general education, comprising history, literature and the law, on top of the maritime skills they would learn.

## Crossing the Line

On 5 September, Mrs Graham notes looking forward to the ceremony of 'crossing the line'. This time-honoured event marked a ship's traversing of the equator. She revealed that some captains, perhaps disturbed by the resulting lack of discipline, paid seamen not to perform the ceremony. But as she notes, 'All work and no play, makes Jack a dull boy'.

Nonetheless, the crew, calling themselves 'Britain's sons', wrote to the captain in advance requesting permission to perform the ceremony, and Thomas Graham was happy to allow it.

Traditionally, a senior crewman dressed himself as Neptune, king of the ocean, and came on board to assume control of the ship. He was accompanied by his family: Amphitrite, his consort, and Triton, their son, who sported a man's body but a fish's tail. Their entourage included seahorses, a footman, constables and, most particularly, a group of barbers whose job it was to shave all new initiates into Neptune's realm.

They sailed on with variable weather for 12 days which gave the crew time to prepare for their festivities. Then on 17 September at about 6 pm, the officer of the watch was informed that there was a mysterious boat alongside bearing lights, and permission was sought to shorten sail and bring the *Doris* to a halt. The captain immediately came on deck, and then:

'Triton mounted upon a seahorse, admirably represented, appeared as bearer of a letter containing the names of all who had not yet crossed the line, and who were consequently to be initiated into the mysteries of the Water God. Triton having thus executed his commission, rode off, and was seen no more till 8 o'clock this morning, when Neptune being announced, the captain went on deck to receive him.

First came Triton mounted as before, then a company of sea-gods or constables dressed in oakum and swabs, but having their arms and shoulders bare, excepting the paint which bedaubed them. Neptune with trident and crown, Amphitrite by his side, and their son at their feet, appeared in a car drawn by eight seahorses, and driven by a sea god: the train followed in the persons of the lawyers, barbers and painters. The whole pageant was well dressed, and going in procession, fully as picturesque as any antique triumphal or religious ceremony; the fine forms of some of the actors struck me exceedingly. I never saw marble more beautiful than some of the backs and shoulders displayed; and the singular clothing to imitate fishes instead of legs, and seaweed skirts, which they had all adopted, carried one back for centuries to the time when all this was religion.

After the progress round the decks, a conference with the captain, and a libation in the form of a glass of brandy, to which the god and goddess vied with each other in devotion, the merriment began. Mock-shaving, or a fine paid, was necessary to admit the newcomers to the good graces of their watery father; and while he was superintending the business, all the rest of the ship's company, officers and all, proceeded to duck each other unmercifully. None but women escaped, and that only by staying in my cabin. The officer of the watch, sentries, quartermasters, and such as are absolutely necessary to look after the ship, are of course held sacred; so that some order is still preserved. It seemed really that "madness ruled the hour"; but at the appointed moment, half past eleven, all ceased: by noon, everybody was at his duty, the decks were dried, and the ship restored to her wonted good order.'

Versions of this ceremony have persisted through the centuries as a right of initiation on Royal Navy and merchant navy ships alike. But they have, and still are, performed in a modified way for passengers' entertainment on board ocean liners that cross the equator. In a similar account of the ceremony, another naval author, John Bechervaise, who played the part of Neptune on HMS *Blossom* in 1825, gives a more detailed description of the shaving of Neptune's initiates:

'The first of the ship's company that were shaved, who was brought up blindfolded by the whole posse of constables, was the armourer... On this man then the barber had to perform his first functions; a bucket was filled with all the cleanings of the hen coops, pig-sties, etc and with it a due proportion of tar had been mixed; with a large paint brush dipped in this villainous compound, and his razor close to him, the barber stood waiting the signal.

My first question was: "What is your name my man?" "John S----, your honour," at the instant of his opening his mouth the brush went across it, when the face the poor creature made is impossible to describe: "Phoo, what do you call that?" I again asked the old man how old he was: "Eight and twenty your honour, and so I am; oh I will spake no more, I will spake no more."

As a last effort to make him open his mouth, I said if you mean to put him overboard, mind have a good rope round him for perhaps he cannot swim. Terrified at the idea of being thrown overboard, the poor fellow said: "I cannot swim, oh, I cannot swim," but as the brush again crossed his mouth, he uttered with his teeth closed: "I will spake no more, by Jesus I will spake no more if you drown me." Amid a roar of laughter two men tripped the handspike on which he sat and sent him backward into the sail [filled with water] where the bear was waiting to receive him; it was soon over, he escaped and stood by to see his shipmates share his fate'.

Usually the weather near the equator provoked what Mrs Graham called, 'long tiresome calms', the so-called Doldrums, with a glassy sea and high heat. But contrary to expectation, the *Doris* had fresh breezes every day, during which they saw lots of fish on the surface, and thunder and lightning at night. Out at sea, Mrs Graham confesses, the lightning would make anyone feel rather vulnerable.

## Reaching Brazil

Taking advantage of favourable winds, the ship cut through the water towards the coast of South America. On 20 September a seaman, Martin Mullins, fell overboard from the topsail yard. The captain put the ship about and tried to launch the cutter to save him but he drowned before rescuers could arrive. Sometimes men falling from a ship hit part of the structure on the way down, but even if they landed in the water unhurt, many sailors could not swim. A sailor falling overboard in the frenzied activity of a storm might not even be missed for hours.

The following day, the *Doris* came within sight of the low and green shores of Brazil. The weather was squally and there was a heavy swell; several times they fired a gun to summon a pilot to navigate them to the unfamiliar harbour of Pernambuco but none was forthcoming. When the port's commodore came on board the next day, they were informed that there was a civil uprising and effectively a state of siege existed.

Mrs Graham was not able to set foot on shore until things had settled down, but after allowing her a few excursions to safe locations, the captain ordered the *Doris* to head away from Pernambuco on 14 October.

They made their way down the coast, stopping firstly at Salvador where the senior officers were entertained by the British consul, but where many troubles awaited the unwary. Civil strife in the city kept threatening to erupt and several sailors deserted the ship. The high heat and ten days of incessant heavy showers of rain were blamed by Mrs Graham for inducing illness. Writing on 16 November, she explained:

'Several of our young people and I myself have begun to feel the bad effects of exposing ourselves too much to the sun and the rain. Yesterday I was so unwell as to put on a blister for cough and pain in my side, and several of the others have slight degrees of fever. But generally speaking, the ship's company has been remarkably healthy.'

But perhaps Mrs Graham had spoken too soon, for that same day she was forced to write: 'Captain Graham taken suddenly and alarmingly ill'. He became a little better by evening, but had to exert himself to deal with an incident that involved two crew of the visiting HMS *Morgiana* being stabbed after a drunken quarrel on shore, and this seemed to make him worse. Mrs Graham tended to her husband and other ill members of the crew as best she could but was ill herself. It seems to have been some sort of infection, but the medical details are so scant that it is difficult to ascertain a diagnosis.

One of the midshipmen was so gravely ill that she took him into her own cabin to look after. On 22 November she wrote:

'At length all the invalids, excepting myself, are better; but, with another blister on, I can do little but write, or look from the cabin windows; and when I do look, I am sure to see something disagreeable. This very moment, there is a slave ship discharging her cargo, and the slaves are singing as they go ashore. They have left the ship, and they see they will be on the dry land; and so, at the command of their keeper, they are singing one of their country songs, in a strange land. Poor wretches! Could they foresee the slave-market, and the separations of friends and relations that will take place there, and the march up the country, and the labour of the mines, and the sugar-works, their singing would be a wailing cry.'

Salvador was the principal slave port in Brazil, and Mrs Graham was writing 12 years before an Act of Parliament abolished slavery in most of the British Empire. Leaving Salvador on 9 December, with local merchants now feeling 'quite safe', the *Doris* continued south to Rio de Janeiro. Six days later, the ship dropped anchor in this most beautiful of locations:

> 'Lofty mountains, rocks of clustered columns, luxuriant wood, bright flowery islands, green banks, all mixed with white buildings; each little eminence crowned with its church or fort; ships at anchor or in motion; and innumerable boats flitting about in such a delicious climate – combine to render Rio de Janeiro the most enchanting scene that imagination can conceive.'

A long stay here was planned, so Mrs Graham rented a house for three weeks. The health of the crew fluctuated: 'Some of our invalids have been gaining ground; others who were well have become invalids'. Meanwhile the political situation in Brazil deteriorated as the population strove to assert independence whilst Portuguese troops were still based there. This unstable situation upset local merchants who repeatedly asked Captain Graham to stay and protect them. The *Doris* maintained a presence and, while revolution continued ashore, the unflappable British even hosted a dance on board ship for dignitaries in the vicinity.

HMS *Aurora* arrived to replace the *Doris*, and Captain Graham returned to Salvador to ensure the situation there was still stable. This busy naval activity at key Brazilian ports was designed to reassure local merchants, but also to make clear to all forces in Brazil that the British were determined to actively protect their trading interests. Arriving back at Salvador on 8 February, everything seemed quiet and so they returned to Rio where Portuguese troops were forced to evacuate by sea.

Captain Graham's health fluctuated considerably from one week to the next and he was often unable to leave the ship. In addition to his feverish illness, he also suffered from gout. But many of the other officers and crew were ill and Mrs Graham helped attend to them as best she could – often taking very little sleep.

On 10 March, the *Doris* left Rio to round Cape Horn and visit Valparaiso in Chile, where it was hoped the milder climate might improve the health of everyone on board. Rounding the Cape was a gruelling and often dangerous undertaking. Within two weeks of sailing south, the temperature had dropped from 33°C at Rio, to 7°C, and Mrs Graham lit a fire in her cabin. The wind blew hard and the swell became heavy, and this made life on board challenging:

> 'I look within, round my little home in the cabin, and every roll of the ship causes accidents irresistibly ludicrous; and in spite of the inconveniences they bring with them, one cannot choose but laugh. Sometimes, in spite of all usual precautions, of cushions and clothes, the breakfast-table is suddenly stripped of half its load, which is lodged in the lee scuppers, whither the coal-scuttle and its contents had adjourned the instant before.'

But there was also a certain exhilaration to be found from their situation: 'We are in the midst of a dark boisterous sea; over us, a dense, grey, cold sky... yet there is a pleasure in stemming the apparently irresistible waves, and in wrestling thus with the elements.'

Fortunately, cold weather seemed to aid the recovery of many of the sick, although not Captain Graham and the first lieutenant, who had also become ill. By 28 March it was cold enough for snow. They had seen many birds around the ship – petrels, albatrosses, even penguins – and there were plenty of whales.

As the temperature plummeted below zero, a hard gale blew up and the dangerous, icy conditions triggered accidents amongst the crew. Mrs Graham and her maid made gloves for the men at the wheel. 'The snow and hail squalls are very severe; ice forms in every fold of the sails. This is hard upon the men, so soon after leaving Rio in the hottest part of the year'.

The weather moderated on 1 April, and shortly afterwards Mrs Graham saw her first iceberg. At this point she reveals that although she kept a diary for the next 18 days, she could not bear to share it and decided not to include the entries in the published version of her journal, for her husband was sinking fast. Her anguish and suffering was made worse by the long dark nights and stormy weather, and during one particular gale, the leading officer's observations in the log of the *Doris* on Sunday, 9 April 1822, record the sadly inevitable: '2.30 am: Departed this life our much esteemed captain'.

The whole log entry for this day is edged in thick black inky borders to indicate the melancholy of the crew. After her husband died, Mrs Graham suddenly realised she was exhausted from continually tending the sick, and undressed herself for bed: 'All was then over, and I slept long and rested; but I awoke to the consciousness of being alone, and a widow, with half the globe between me and my kindred'.

What killed Captain Graham and affected his crew so badly? It is impossible to know without more details of the symptoms, and there are a number of possibilities. Yet it seems to have been an infection that produced a long period of illness and was fatal in only a minority of sufferers, so yellow fever is perhaps the most likely cause since it notoriously affected the coast of South America.

Many of the crew were kind to Mrs Graham but she was distraught. On 20 April 1822, the *Doris* arrived at Valparaiso, but it was not until 30 April that Captain Graham was buried. The ship's log records the events of that day:

> '2.30 pm:   The boats of HMS Blossom, and American ships Franklin and Constellation came along to form the funeral procession of Captain Graham. Three boats left the ship for the shore to inter the body. Fired one-minute guns (twenty in number). On the arrival of the body on shore, it was attended by the Governor, the Commodore, and all the officers of the American ships, and the colours of every ship (and nation) half-mast.
>
> 5.30 pm:   Hoisted the colours.
>
> 6.30 pm:   Boats returned on board.'

Poor Mrs Graham was utterly bereft. She elected to leave the ship at Chile and not to return to England immediately; and could not be persuaded otherwise. Mrs Graham spent time there in solace, cutting herself off from others. Her parting line to the readers of her published journal was: 'My comfort must come from Him who in his own time will "wipe off all tears from our faces".'

However, she survived and did eventually return to England where she later remarried.

*Chapter Seven*

# Early Steamship Across the Atlantic

## *(1844, George Moore, SS* **Great Western***)*

The steamship revolutionised the passenger's experience of ocean travel. Steamers were considerably faster than sail and were much more reliable because they didn't depend upon favourable winds, and could make progress even in stormy conditions. Early innovators, however, had met with some scepticism. Napoleon famously remarked: 'You would make a ship sail against the winds and currents by lighting a bonfire under her deck... I have no time for such nonsense'.

Before the advent of steam, during the era of sail, many ships departed simply when they were 'ready' – usually when all the cargo was aboard. Yet some companies began to offer a regular sailing schedule with fixed times of departure: the American company Black Ball Line was the first, starting before 1820 and departing on a fixed day each month, but the contrariness of the weather remained a problem. However, steam made regular sailing schedules much more achievable and they soon became the norm. Passengers now knew when their ship was due to depart and when it would arrive at its destination: they could book in advance with some confidence in their itinerary. Such regularly scheduled ships were initially called 'packets' because they often carried the mail, but by the end of the nineteenth century they were called liners.

## Brunel's Ship

SS *Great Western* was designed by Isambard Kingdom Brunel, and was the first ship built for the purpose of crossing the Atlantic using a steam engine as the principal means of propulsion. The owners proudly dubbed it 'the first steamship which has ever traversed and returned across the Atlantic, between England and the United States, by the powers of machinery exercised unceasingly throughout the whole distance'. Other steam vessels had crossed the ocean before, most notably the American ship *Savannah*, as far back as 1819. However, *Savannah* had been a sailing ship that used its engines for only a small proportion of the journey, and it had not been a commercial success.

The engine on *Great Western* drove a large paddlewheel on each side of the hull and, despite being a steamship, the vessel still carried four masts. The sails offered an alternative means of propulsion in case of engine failure, and in fact steamships continued to carry both engines and sails until the late 1880s, reflecting the maritime profession's inability to trust completely to steam power. Sails also had the useful function of steadying the ship in bad weather.

Brunel's ship made its maiden Atlantic voyage from Bristol in 1838 and at the time of its launch was the largest ship in the world. Right up to its maiden voyage, some people had doubted that steam-powered ships were a practical and safe alternative to sail. Yet the nation was soon amazed that you could now cross the Atlantic in as little as twelve days, instead of at least a month under sail, and often nearer to six weeks. As a result *Great Western* drew enormous public interest and media coverage: even the captain's and engineer's logs of the maiden voyage were published to meet the widespread enthusiasm amongst the public to find out more.

The *Great Western*'s engines meant she could achieve an average speed of around nine knots all the way across. However, ship designers had not at this period fully embraced the concept of metal hulls, so *Great Western* was a wooden ship.

## The Passenger Experience

George Moore was a self-made businessman and philanthropist from Cumberland. At the age of 38 he took a voyage on *Great Western* to visit North America, for which he paid a fare of 35 guineas. His ship left Liverpool on 17 August 1844, with 138 passengers and a crew of around 60.

The size of the *Great Western* allowed it to have a large cabin block on the upper deck that was nearly 60 feet long, as well as cabins below decks. The accommodation was better than that provided by the sailing ships of the period but was still very basic and cramped in the light of what was to come in the next 50 years. Moore's cabin was only around seven feet by eight feet, with two bunks that could be folded up against the wall. However, there were some nods to elegance not seen before. For example, passengers could call a steward to their room by using a bell rope, and the saloon was beautifully decorated with original painted panels depicting country scenes, and representations of arts, sciences and sports.

Two years previously, Charles Dickens had travelled on a similar ship, Cunard's SS *Britannia*, and described his cabin as an 'utterly impracticable, thoroughly hopeless and profoundly preposterous box':

'We all by common consent agreed that this state-room was the pleasantest and most facetious and capital contrivance possible; and that to have had it one inch larger would have been quite a disagreeable and deplorable state of things. And with this, and with showing how – by very nearly closing the door and twining in and out like serpents, and by counting the little washing slab as standing-room – we could manage to insinuate four people into it, all at one time; and entreating each other to observe how very airy it was (in dock), and how there was a beautiful porthole which could be kept open all day (weather permitting), and how there was quite a large bull's-eye just over the looking-glass which would render shaving a perfectly easy and delightful process (when the ship didn't roll too much); we arrived, at last, at the unanimous conclusion that it was rather spacious than otherwise. Though I do verily believe that, deducting the two berths, one above the other, than which nothing smaller for sleeping in was ever made except coffins, it was no bigger than one of those hackney cabriolets which have the door behind, and shoot their fares out like sacks of coals upon the pavement.'

Another author, Reverend Balch, describes the appearance of Moore's ship to a new passenger:

'The Great Western is, so to speak, three stories high forward and aft, and two in the 'waist' or middle of the ship: aft there is the lower storey or cabin, above it the saloon – the roof or covering of which is the quarterdeck and may, for the purposes of description, be considered as a third storey. In the waist, or middle, the lower storey is occupied by the engine room, the roof or covering of which is the main deck. On this main deck, in the centre, are placed the chimney, galleys, and icehouse; the various offices appertaining to the stewards and police of the ship at the sides. This part is open above, and protected by the wheel-houses and sides of the ship which rise to the height of fourteen feet.'

The *Great Western* ran into a strong north-westerly gale as soon as it had cleared land, and Moore reveals that within two hours of leaving port, very few passengers could bear to be on deck. It was a new experience for many travellers to be on a ship that simply ploughed on through the stormy waters, rather than taking in sail and riding out the bad weather as sailing vessels had been forced to do in the past. The steamship would have pitched and rolled in a manner that must have seemed alarming, and the decks would have been frequently deluged with sea, but *Great Western* carried on regardless. By 7 o'clock, Moore himself had had enough and 'went to bed rather squeamish'.

An all-pervading part of the passenger experience on *Great Western* was the sound of the engines driving the two large paddlewheels. It was something you had to get used to as background noise. Moore was wakened early the next morning when the noise suddenly stopped. Engine trouble. It took an hour-and-a-half to fix, but then they were on their way once more.

As voyages from most eras bear witness, the passengers' daily activities on a ship are inevitably structured around mealtimes. Thus Moore soon discovered that the routine of each day would be as follows: 'The gong sounds at half-past seven to rise; breakfast at nine; at twelve lunch; at half-past three dress for dinner; at four dine; half-past seven tea; very few take supper at ten; lights put out at eleven punctually'.

The lights, of course, were candle lamps as there was no electricity on board. The crewmen designated to look after the sufficiency and safety of this lighting were thus called lamp-trimmers. The 60-odd crewmen were headed by Captain Matthews and his deputy, the first mate. Being a steamship, there was also a chief engineer. It was the speed of the ship that attracted the passengers and George Moore, rather helpfully, kept a log of the distances that the *Great Western* travelled each day:

| Date | Nautical miles |
| --- | --- |
| Sunday, 18 August 1844 | 165 |
| Monday, 19 | 211 |
| Tuesday, 20 | 193 |
| Wednesday, 21 | 228 |
| Thursday, 22 | 220 |
| Friday, 23 | 259 |
| Saturday, 24 | 239 |
| Sunday, 25 | 211 |
| Monday, 26 | 212 |
| Tuesday, 27 | 209 |
| Wednesday, 28 | 229 |
| Thursday, 29 | 200 |

Thus the *Great Western* travelled an average of 212 miles every day at a speed of around 9 knots, but the ship's top speed was nearer 11 knots.

Ship owners and passengers alike were so wrapped up in the new-found speed of ocean travel under steam that little thought was given to passenger comforts for some time. Even though the décor was comfortable, it was plain by later standards. Part of the problem was that, being a comparatively small ship, space generally was at a premium. The *Great Western* had been very expensive to build, so to make it commercially viable, every inch was devoted to generating income from housing passengers or cargo, which left little room for much else. It took a few decades for ship owners to realise that passengers wanted more than a quick voyage – they wanted to be comfortable and entertained, and they would pay for the privilege.

Thus there were few facilities on board *Great Western* to distract the passengers. The ship had no shops or salons. There was no swimming pool, tennis court, gym, nor even a library; there was no band, no concerts, parties or dances. George Moore's account is interesting precisely because it reveals the monotony of comparatively fast but dull ocean travel. Compare this to the entertainments and diversions offered on board ships in the late nineteenth and twentieth centuries.

Meanwhile in 1844, George Moore devised his own daily schedule to while away the time between meals:

> 'Rise at half-past seven; walk on deck till breakfast; read at least six chapters in the Bible the first thing after breakfast; then walk on deck for an hour till lunch; afterwards write for an hour; then walk on deck for another hour; then read any books I have till dinner; between dinner and tea walk and talk, and take stock of the passengers, being some of all sorts here; after tea whist till ten, and then turn in.'

Not a very inspiring daily routine, perhaps, for two weeks at sea. Card-playing games such as whist were popular in Victorian England but gambling was frowned upon by many Christian groups. As the voyage progressed, George Moore observed, 'Some heavy card-playing on board, and imprudent losses, which I much regretted to see'.

Within a week, this lack of variation in his day-to-day activities clearly led to boredom. His brief diary entry for Saturday, 24 August reflects this: 'Read; talked; walked; lunched; walked, and read again. At nine, drank [to] "wives and sweethearts"; and then to bed'. And later entries are often curtailed merely to 'spent the day as usual'. By the end of the voyage, Moore admitted he was 'heartily sick of the Atlantic'.

However, there were occasional breaks from the daily monotony. On each Sunday morning, for example, a church service took place. Their first worship was without a sermon because there was no clergyman on board, and Moore noted that only about half the passengers attended, but on the second Sunday an American passenger read a sermon from a book. Moore also remarks that some of the passengers occasionally sang for entertainment and he heard 'some German, Irish, English and Yankee songs'.

All passengers spend some time enjoying the relaxing pastime of sea-watching – observing the coast at the beginning and end of the voyage; other ships, and wildlife such as porpoises and whales. But the ability to do this was heavily affected by the weather; the sun brought everyone out on deck, the storms sent them scurrying below, while the four days of fog as they approached Newfoundland lowered everyone's spirits as they could see nothing – it was in Moore's own words 'dark, cold, and comfortless'. The weather could also interfere with passengers' other basic shipboard activities. For example, a particularly stormy spell during the voyage prevented Moore from being able to write a word – and presumably he couldn't walk the decks either – and that lasted three days.

Captain Matthews was to take the *Great Western* through many storms in his career. A particularly dramatic one in 1846 ripped away lifeboats and parts of the ship such as the icehouse, flooded the saloon and cabins, and left passengers convinced their number was up. This was the subject of a book by Reverend Balch and two other ministers, who saw the hand of God in their survival, yet publications of this nature did help reassure readers of the safety of steamships in dramatic conditions – and indeed, in certain circumstances, their (perhaps) greater safety than sail.

However, in 1844 George Moore describes one particular evening where the skies, for once, made a very favourable impression on him: 'We had the most brilliant sunset I ever saw: it was past all description! It gave me a good impression of an American sun. The Yankees broke out into applause, and welcomed the face of Sol as that of an old and tried friend'.

## Dining on Board

Whatever else the limitations associated with being at sea in 1844, dining does not seem to have been one of them. There were, of course, no electric cookers and all the hot food had to be cooked on open fire stoves. On Thursday, 29 August, passengers enjoyed a 'grand state-dinner', and Moore summarises the plentiful bill of fare for the occasion:

## BREAKFAST

| | |
|---|---|
| Beefsteaks | Omelettes |
| Mutton Chops | Boiled Eggs |
| Pork Chops | Hominy |
| Ham and Eggs | Hash |
| Fried Bacon | Mush |
| Fricassée Chicken | Fried Fish (Soles) |
| Veal Cutlets | Fried Potatoes |
| Stews | |

## DINNER

| | |
|---|---|
| Mock Turtle Soup | Boiled Fowls |
| Boiled Salmon & Lobster Sauce | Corned Beef |
| Baked Fish | Corned Pork |
| Roast Beef | Ham |
| Saddles of Mutton | Tongues |
| Roast Lamb | Fricandeau |
| Roast Turkey | Mutton Cutlets |
| Roast Veal | Macaroni |
| Roast Pig | Curry |
| Olive Ducks | Irish Stew |
| Roast Fowls | Calf's Head |
| Roast Geese | Roast Hare |
| Boiled Mutton | Lobster Patties |
| Galantine Turkey | Chicken Salad |

## PASTRY

| | |
|---|---|
| Plum Pudding | Mince Pies |
| Apple Dumpling | Damson Pies |
| Raspberry Rollers | Cherry Pies |
| Baked Apple Pudding | Rice Pudding |
| Apple Pies | Orange Pudding |
| Cranberry Pies | Custard Pudding |
| Raspberry Puffs | Beignets |
| Plum Pies | Brandy Fruits |
| plus wines, jellies and blancmanges | |

The dining arrangements comprised a series of large tables where everyone sat together and were served at the table. Where possible, the captain attended the passengers' dinner in person. The captain of the *Great Western* was Barnard Matthews, whom Moore describes as 'a gentlemanly, courteous, obliging little fellow'. This was his first voyage as ship's master, he having been first mate to the previous commander, James Hosken, since the vessel's launch.

At the end of the grand dinner the passengers presented Captain Matthews 'with a memorial signed by all the passengers', although Moore noted afterwards that their captain 'richly deserved a more substantial mark of our regard for his unremitting attentions'.

Although this special meal seems to have been a success, on other occasions seasickness sometimes kept passengers from the dining table. On 23 August for example, Moore describes the effects of a long ocean swell that set the ship rolling: 'A very small muster at breakfast. The ladies generally ill... During dinner all the sails taken in; and the heavy pitching of the ship sent all the grumblers from the table'.

## Arrival

As the ship neared the end of the voyage, the passengers began to prepare for their departure. Drinks were not included in the fare, so Moore had to settle his wine bill with the head steward. He also finished his letters to friends and family back in England so that they might catch the mail ship returning across the Atlantic.

His last day on board was Saturday, 31 August, which began with a beautiful morning that brought all the passengers out on deck to enjoy the sunshine. A pilot boat came out to offer its services in navigating the *Great Western* to its New York berth:

'The pilot (who had come out 160 miles to get the job, a very intelligent fellow) lent me a New York paper. A good many vessels in sight. Came close to Long Island. All bustle and confusion packing. Our boat did her best, but we saw we should be too late for the mail [ship]. Got to Sandy Hook at five; the Narrows at six; and up the East River at seven. Passed Fort Hamilton; and at half-past seven landed in New York.'

Moore couldn't wait to leave the *Great Western*, yet suddenly the ship was all hustle and bustle. The passengers were gathered and anxious to depart, the crew was hurrying to secure the vessel safely, the port officials were on the quay to receive the ship, and a crowd of relatives, friends and sightseers were assembled on shore to welcome them.

The custom-house officers would not allow any luggage to be landed after sunset, so despite all Moore's preparation for disembarking, he had to leave his possessions behind on the ship and collect them the next morning. They were warned to be careful as they departed because 'hundreds of pickpockets were on the lookout'.

Nonetheless, George Moore was able to walk down the gangplank safely and made his way to a nearby hotel: 'We sojourned at the Astor House Hotel. Had a warm-bath, and retired to rest, grateful that I was once more on *Terra firma*'.

His passage altogether had been 3,022 miles in just 14 days.

## Chapter Eight

# Death and Disease Under Sail

## *(1847, William Smith, India)*

The advent of steamships, that began in earnest in the 1840s, allowed wealthy people such as George Moore to cross the Atlantic in two weeks or less. However, for impoverished emigrant passengers, sail remained the principal means of ocean travel for some time because of its affordability. As the nineteenth century progressed and steamships predominated, eventually even the poorest emigrants could journey by steamer. In Chapter 13, for example, there is an account of emigrants on the SS *Lucania* in 1896.

Yet the 1840s was still the heyday of emigrant travel under sail, and in 1847, William Smith chose the sailing ship *India* to emigrate to America. He was an unemployed weaver who had struggled for years to escape the poverty trap without success, so he left his wife and child in Manchester and sought employment in the United States.

### Delays and Deceit

Smith booked passage in the *India*'s steerage and was due to depart Liverpool on 12 November 1847. There was a crew of 24 under Captain Thompson and first mate Connor, and about 300 passengers. Surprisingly, there are many similarities between the conditions encountered by the emigrants on the *India* and those on the *Mayflower* nearly 230 years before (Chapter 2). Passengers were crammed on board with little personal space, there was no ship's surgeon, and the only food provided was a small ration of ship's biscuits. So, as in the *Mayflower*, passengers had to bring their own provisions for the voyage, or else virtually starve.

Departure times for sailing vessels could still be extremely unreliable in 1847, as both the *Mayflower* passengers and Henry Fielding discovered in earlier centuries. The *India* was detained ten days waiting for cargo, and then a further day when the vessel sprang a leak.

The deceitfulness of the ship owners towards their fare-paying passengers, as witnessed by Janet Schaw's family in the 1770s, was soon in evidence on the *India* as well. The lateness of departure meant that passengers ate into provisions brought for the voyage and so they petitioned the company to pay one shilling per day sustenance, which the law permitted them to claim during a delay. The ship owners refused but relented when the passengers sought a government agent to help them, and agreed to pay every passenger 11 shillings to buy more food. However, as soon as the agent left, the unscrupulous owners paid a mere two shillings, gave the passengers some ship's biscuits, and towed the *India* so far from shore that they could not contact the government agent. Here the furious passengers remained for a further two days 'during which time there was great confusion and uproar on board'.

On Friday, 26 November they at last set sail: 14 days late. Despite the delays and unpleasantness, Smith found himself crying as the shores of his homeland receded.

## Into the Ocean

As soon as *India* headed out to sea, Smith began to feel seasick: 'It reduced me so much that I could not walk without assistance, for I felt as weak as an infant'. And for two days he retired below decks. On the third day he emerged into the open air and was delighted to see a beautiful blue sky and the ship surrounded by the boundless expanse of the ocean. The *India* was making good headway too: 'The ship was running like a racehorse, coursing over the waters with a speed that promised to bring us quickly to our journey's end'.

However, this fine beginning was not to last. All too soon, the ship met contrary winds which frustrated their progress. Inevitably, this being winter, they encountered a major storm that lasted 'four days and five nights'. It began with torrential rain, and gradually the wind increased in force until the mate ordered all the hatches fastened down, leaving the passengers confined below decks in the semi-darkness. This was necessary to stop the heavy seas breaking over the ship from flooding the vessel, but for passengers trapped in the cramped gloom it was frightening:

'The increasing violence of the storm, the moaning and creaking of the ship, the howling of the wind and the roaring of the waves, was horrible to those not accustomed to such scenes; and every few minutes a wave would strike the ship with such force as to make it tremble beneath us, causing a shock so great that at every blow we expected to see the bow stave in and the ship sink.'

A few candle lanterns dangled above their heads providing a weak, glimmering light in the blackness. In the middle of the night, and to make matters worse, a number of boxes and barrels broke loose in the dark and thundered amongst the passengers. In no time, this stray cargo had smashed everything it came into contact with – scattering the passengers' belongings everywhere.

'The cries of the women and children was heart-rending; some praying, others weeping bitterly, as they saw their provisions and clothes (the only property they possessed) destroyed. The passengers being sea-sick, were vomiting in all parts of the vessel; the heat became intense in consequence of the hatchways being closed down... The scent arising from the matter vomited up, and from other causes, became intolerable.'

During the storm, the passengers were unable to light a fire and so had to survive on cold water and ship's biscuits alone. Eventually, after four days, the hatchways were opened to allow them back on deck, but the stampede to escape the oppressive, polluted atmosphere caused several severe injuries.

About 3 am the next morning the passengers were awakened by an alarmingly loud crash as the foremast – weakened in the storm – suddenly toppled down above their heads. Racing up on deck, Smith found chaos: 'The scene which met my eye upon reaching the deck was awful. Broken fragments of the foremast, rigging, chains etc, were strewn from one end to the other'.

### Accidents at Sea

Later the same day, while the deck was still being cleared, a young sailor fell from the yardarm into the water. The cry of 'man overboard' ran through the ship, but despite searching for him, he was never seen again. As noted previously, most sailors could not swim and even if they could, the *India*'s crew were weakened by a four-day period of almost continual duty during the storm, and poor rations. Smith was deeply shocked at the death because he had enjoyed the sailor's company, and, 'this sad accident caused a general gloom among the passengers'.

The next day, Smith went up on deck to wash himself using a bucket of water. A ladder provided the means of returning below, but Smith climbed down when it was wet and slippery. With his coat folded over one arm, he couldn't hold on properly and tumbled to the deck below, cracking his head on a box which knocked him out.

> 'Upon returning to consciousness I saw the captain, first mate, and several sailors around me, with my head bandaged, and my shirt collar and bosom covered with blood from a wound in my left temple, the mark of which I shall carry to my grave. I was in great agony from the pains in my head and sides.'

Smith was confined to bed for several days and during this time there was a third accident. A 14-year-old boy had been lying, dozing, on the forecastle. Suddenly a gust of wind filled the jib which snapped taut, whip-cracking a loose rope attached to it which caught the boy about the head. The force of the blow nearly took off his scalp, leaving a deep bloody cut all the way around his skull. 'The captain held him, while the first mate sewed up the wound, during which painful operation the boy did not utter a scream or even a murmur'.

Passenger ships at this time were not obliged to carry a surgeon, whilst on naval ships they were compulsory, where they devoted much time to treating trauma: gashes, broken bones, hernias and so forth. But these three accidents were just the beginning of the ordeal for passengers on the *India*.

## Ship Fever

After nearly four weeks at sea, Smith found himself on deck wondering at the peaceful ocean and warm weather. Yet in the time it had taken the *India* to reach halfway across the Atlantic, a steamer of the period could have travelled all the way to America and back again. It was nearly Christmas, thought Smith, so shouldn't it have been colder by now? On investigation, it transpired that Captain Thompson had opted for a more southerly course to avoid further storms, as well as the icebergs which notoriously inhabited the wintry northern Atlantic.

Smith became concerned that warm weather would encourage the spread of ship fever which had already affected a few passengers. This disease, now known as typhus, became a principal scourge of seagoing travellers in the nineteenth century. Typhus is a bacterial infection spread by lice, and which manifests itself where people are in close proximity, such as prisons, hospitals and, of course, ships. Within these environments, lice can move easily from one human to another, either via personal contact or by moving from, for example, a person's bedding onto a new host. The lice's bite infects recipients with the typhus bacteria.

Soon, passengers and crew began to succumb to ship fever in greater numbers. The initial symptoms were aptly summarised by naval surgeon Robert Robertson:

'The diagnostic symptoms, or those which generally introduce the fever, are rigors or chilliness, or alternate chills and heats; sickness at stomach, headache, universal pains (or as the sick express it: 'pains all over them') or pains in all their bones but especially in the loins or back, and a morbid appearance in the countenance.'

The pains increased as the patient's condition deteriorated and were soon accompanied by a fever that made victims intensely hot and dehydrated. The ship fever sufferer was by this stage sweaty, thirsty, shivery, weak and hoarse-voiced. He or she may also have had a cough, and sometimes pains in their eyes, bones and muscles. There was also a characteristic rash of small red spots.

Although some sufferers slowly improved, the infection was often fatal with a terminal course commonly heralded by frenzied behaviour, excitable ranting or delirium. Eventually the poor souls became unconscious, then died. The whole illness could take as long as two weeks to carry the victim off.

Soon enough, ship fever claimed its first fatality, and a horror-struck Smith described the funeral:

> 'When a death occurs, the body is enveloped in canvas, and sewed up with about forty or fifty pounds of stone, which are fastened at the feet, for the purpose of causing the body to sink deep in the ocean. The corpse is then brought on deck and extended upon a plank; the Union Jack flag is then spread over the body, and the plank is put on the rail at the gangway. All hands are called to witness the solemn scene, and every head is uncovered. The captain then reads the funeral service, and as he reads the words "we commit the body to the deep", the plank is raised, and the body is launched into the bosom of the ocean.'

The whole scene made a very deep impression on him: 'To hear the earth thrown upon a coffin in a churchyard is sufficiently appalling, but not as bad as this awful plunge into the deep. The first time I saw this sight it so shocked my feelings that I felt the blood run cold through my veins'.

By the fifth week at sea, they had condemned 15 passengers to the deep as a result of ship fever, and a further 42 were seriously ill. Members of the crew succumbed too, and the next week Captain Thompson himself died. He and Connor, the first mate, had visited the ill passengers regularly and shown them great kindness, but frequent close contact with victims had greatly increased their chances of infection. Sadly, it had been Captain Thompson's last voyage, after which he had planned to retire to spend time with his family.

The slowness of the ship's progress and the demands of the sick meant that the water supply had to be rationed. They also discovered that four of the ship's water caskets had not been filled before departure. Consequently, Connor, now the new captain, allowed each person a pint of water per day, and rations of ship's biscuits were halved.

When they spotted a ship heading to Dublin, the *India*'s crew and passengers hoped they might beg or buy more food and water. However, when within speaking distance, her captain explained he could spare them no provisions because half his own crew were sick with ship fever and more than half his passengers had already died of it. A second ship, encountered shortly afterwards, could also spare nothing.

The passengers who weren't ill began to imagine they would all die of thirst, whilst they watched with misery and despair as more people died of the fever:

> 'The scenes I witnessed daily were indeed awful: to hear the heart-rending cries of wives at the loss of their husbands, the agonies of husbands at the sight of the corpse of their wives, and the lamentations of fatherless and motherless children; brothers and sisters dying, leaving their aged parents without means of support in their declining years. These were sights to melt a heart of stone. I saw the tear of sympathy run down the cheek of many a hardened sailor.'

Most of those who died from ship fever became delirious: 'One day there were three men walking about the ship raving mad,' Smith says. The first believed he was a priest 'and told the passengers they would all die and go to hell unless they permitted him to make the sign of the cross and baptise them'. The second believed he was in New York, and whilst unsupervised threw himself overboard and was drowned. The third tried to stab his wife and became so aggressive that he had to be tied down: 'His wife said he was a kind and affectionate husband until seized with the fever'. This last man, miraculously, survived.

However, Captain Connor instituted new rules for delirious patients: if they were violent they would be tied down and were not allowed on deck. He posted guards around the ship to make sure these strictures were obeyed.

During all the suffering, Smith witnessed acts of notable kindness. and of enormous selfishness, as perhaps is to be expected amongst a group of people in fear of dying. Some passengers, determined to protect themselves, cut themselves off as much as possible – even from their own family members – whilst others showed great compassion even to ill people they hardly knew, and in so doing put themselves at risk of infection.

## New Threats

As if their existing problems were not enough, passengers and crew alike now faced a new problem – dysentery. Also known as the flux, this disease was caused by contaminated food, or in this case, water. Everyone knew by its taste and appearance that the water was contaminated but they had no other: 'our water' writes Smith, 'was in such a state of decomposition that no human being could drink it, until forced by being placed in similar circumstances with ourselves'.

The ship was now ravaged by two infectious diseases simultaneously: typhus and dysentery. The poor captain experimented with various medicines but to no avail. The passengers became frightened and despondent:

'You may easily conceive the panic this created among us. Such sweeping calamities exercised a baneful influence on the minds of many... despair was depicted in every countenance, and desolation spread throughout the ship. To have a friend well this hour, sick the next, and in a few hours more dead and thrown overboard before his remains are cold, is indeed awful!'

In an account from the same year as that recorded by Smith, 1847, passenger Robert Whyte described an emigrant ship from Ireland beset by fever and dysentery. This was the era of the Great Famine and the Highland Potato Famine; as a result many families from Ireland and Scotland were desperate to leave their homes for the chance of a new life abroad. Already weakened by malnutrition, the crowded conditions on ships readily encouraged the spread of any infection brought on board. The *Quebec Chronicle* for August 1847 recorded example mortality rates on emigrant ships that arrived in Canada on just *one day*. The death rate was nearly one passenger in every 11:

| Vessels | Where from | Passengers aboard | Died of ship fever |
| --- | --- | --- | --- |
| Goliah | Liverpool | 600 | 46 |
| Charles Richards | Sligo | 178 | 8 |
| Medusa | Cork | 194 | 2 |
| Alert | Waterford | 234 | 4 |
| Jordine | Liverpool | 354 | 8 |
| Manchester | Liverpool | 512 | 11 |

| | | | |
|---|---|---|---|
| *Jessie* | Cork | 437 | 37 |
| *Erin's Queen* | Liverpool | 517 | 50 |
| *Sarah* | Liverpool | 248 | 31 |
| *Rosana* | Cork | 254 | 3 |
| *Triton* | Liverpool | 483 | 90 |
| *Thistle* | Liverpool | 389 | 8 |
| *Avon* | Cork | 550 | 136 |
| | | Total = 4950 | Total = 434 |

Government figures estimated that 17,500 British emigrants to Canada died in 1847, the worst year on record: around one third on board ship, the remainder perishing in quarantine or hospitals shortly after arrival. However, these figures are estimates at best, and there are no comparable figures for the USA. Although many thousands suffered, not all vessels were affected. William Fulford emigrated from Devon to Quebec in 1848, along with 55 other passengers on the *Civility*, and none of them experienced more than a cold. Having said this, he does remark that the doctor who inspected them before they disembarked at Quebec pronounced them the most healthy passengers he had ever seen.

Meanwhile on the *India*, most passengers had exhausted their own food supplies by the sixth week, so had only the ship's basic rations of a pound of ship's biscuits and a pint of water per day to live on. The sick needed clean water to replace that which they'd lost from diarrhoea or fevered sweating. But they couldn't have it. When Smith himself eventually fell ill with both dysentery and ship fever, he visited the captain and *begged* for more water, but he was refused.

Smith describes his symptoms in some detail. He became weak and very fatigued on minimal exertion – 'I felt as though I had no life in me' – then came dizziness so that he could not walk for fear of falling. 'I was suffering much from a violent pain in my head, my brains felt as if they were on fire, my tongue clove to the roof of my mouth, and my lips were parched with excessive thirst. Cheerfully, would I have given the world, had I possessed it, for one draught of water'.

Diarrhoea, vomit, sweat, stale clothes and decay created a stench in the steerage which was horrid, but Smith could not leave his berth and go on deck. He hadn't the strength. During this period of extreme weakness, another storm arose and kept the passengers confined below for two miserable, stinking, days in virtual darkness. It was all Smith could do to stop himself from falling out of bed as the ship pitched, rocked and shook. His 'heart was filled with gloomy foreboding' as he imagined his family back at home.

## End in Sight

Once the storm had abated, the passengers were again allowed on deck and Captain Connor came to tend to the sick as best he could. This noble act, which clearly threatened his life, endeared him greatly to the passengers and helped to boost their spirits. In this, their seventh week afloat, they espied a large mass of floating seaweed and Captain Connor assured them this signified land was only a few days away.

However, Smith was still confined to bed, so weak he couldn't even sit up, and unable to eat: 'My eyes were dismal and sunken, and my bones seemed ready to burst through my skin'. Convinced he was dying, he sent for a fellow Mancunian, Felix McQuade, who had himself been ill but was recovering. Smith gave him his last few shillings and asked McQuade to write to his family explaining what had happened to him; this gave Smith great comfort.

Smith's fever abated in the eighth week, so he hoped to see land before he died, or at least not be buried at sea, which horrified him. McQuade stayed with him several hours every day, for Smith was still bed-bound. Captain Connor had not been seen for some days because he too was ill, but one day he struggled down to visit all the ill passengers. Pale, thin and exhausted, the captain's appearance shocked everyone, and he had to lean on the shoulders of two seamen to get around.

'When he reached my berth, he seemed somewhat surprised, and exclaimed, "What, Smith! You alive yet!".

"Yes, sir," said I, "thank God, I am, but I don't think I can live many days longer".

"Don't be down-hearted about that," said he, "for I expect a pilot on board tomorrow, and you will soon be in Staten Island Hospital, where you will have good doctors to attend to you. I see the fever has left you, and if you live to land you will get cured of the dysentery, and perhaps outlive me".

These were the last words he spoke to me, and alas, they proved too prophetic.'

Sure enough, at nine the next morning a pilot arrived to the cheers of all those on board strong enough to give them. The sight of land brought relief, thanks and joy to the survivors: 'Some fell upon their knees and thanked God for his mercy to them; some wept for joy; others capered about, exhibiting extravagant demonstrations of joy'.

On arrival, a US health officer ordered all the sick to hospital and Smith was carried up on deck by two seamen. He looked for Captain Connor to thank him, but he had already been taken ashore where Smith later learned that he died. Twenty-six passengers had been buried at sea, and a further 123 were carried to the hospital in carts, many of them dying. He does not record the number of crew affected, but at least three died.

Despite an appalling lack of care at the hospital, Smith survived. He was convinced that around half of the passengers who boarded at Liverpool died on the *India*, or within a short time of docking, although there are no official figures to back up his estimate. Fortunately, after his shocking ordeal he found profitable and enjoyable employment in America to support his family.

## Chapter Nine

# Christian Missionary to Africa

## *(1858, Rev William Neville, SS Armenian)*

William Latimer Neville was educated at Oxford and was curate at the Church of the Holy Trinity, Brompton, when he learned of a vacancy: Superintendent of the Pongas Mission in Sierra Leone. He applied for this missionary posting in the hope that he 'might thereby be of service in promoting the glory of God and the salvation of souls'. Neville was aware that West Africa was the home of dangerous fevers: indeed it was known as the 'White Man's Grave' because of the prevalence of malaria and yellow fever, to name but two. He also knew that fever had claimed the previous incumbent, Hamble Leacock, known as the 'Martyr of Pongas', and recently a second clergyman, Samuel Higgs. But Neville applied for the job anyway, along with three other hopefuls.

Much to his combined joy and trepidation, Neville's application was successful. He was 56 years of age, single and described as 'of a strong constitution, capable of hard work, and never so well as in hot weather'.

## Departure

Neville was to travel on the 230-feet long steamship SS *Armenian*. This was a fully rigged sailing ship known as a barque, with three masts, but it also sported two comparatively new innovations. The first was a screw propeller driven by a steam engine; the second, an iron hull. Both of these developments had been known about for some years but it was only in the preceding decade that they had been combined for the first time by Brunel in his second ship, SS *Great Britain*.

Iron hulls offered greater strength and durability to the ship's structure, and in a vital foreshadowing of future requirements, metal allowed the construction of much larger vessels than did wood. The propeller had been invented in the 1830s and had many advantages over the paddlewheels that Brunel had adopted for his first pioneering ship, *Great Western*. Propellers were cheaper to build, lighter, and needed smaller engines that took up less space. In practice, the propeller also proved a more efficient means of propulsion than paddlewheels, and offered ships both greater manoeuvrability and improved stability in stormy seas.

On 24 August 1858, Neville boarded the *Armenian* at Plymouth. Departure had been scheduled for 3 pm, but two accidents had caused a delay – an earlier collision with the *Ocean Monarch* had left damage that had to be repaired, and on the morning of sailing, the *Armenian* fell foul of a naval vessel. Collisions amongst ships were common, as Fielding also discovered on his voyage, simply because busy ports and waterways were crowded and vessels were not as easy to control as their modern equivalents. Three hours later than scheduled, the ship was eventually fully prepared to set off.

The captain fired a gun to signal that the ship was ready to leave and all visitors were hurried off the ship, including a colleague of Neville's who had kindly visited him on board. Neville felt a sudden pang of separation as this last friendly face departed, but took comfort in his holy quest. He reported to the purser, George Fidler, his willingness to perform any religious duties required while on board, and accordingly was asked to say grace when the passengers sat down for their first evening meal just a few minutes later. Fidler and two of the stewards serving Neville's meal had been aboard the SS *Candace* three months before when it was wrecked off Gibraltar after colliding with a Dutch ship, and had been lucky to escape with their lives.

Neville was impressed by the fare: 'A plentiful meal was provided – soup, fish, beef, mutton, fowls, pastry etc – everybody seemed to have a good appetite, and dinner passed off without the slightest infringement of the rules of decorum'.

After the meal, his sadness returned at the renewed realisation that he was leaving England. He stood on deck and watched his homeland disappear over the horizon: 'A few tears rolled down my cheeks'.

## Life on Board

The following day, Neville rose after a good night's rest. 'The pitching of the ship, so far from producing sickness, acted like the rocking of a cradle upon a child: it sent me to sleep'. He had the cabin to himself, which was fortunate because it was small, being only eight feet by six feet, yet it accommodated a bunk and provided enough space for his carpet bags and trunks. The *Armenian* would have accommodated passengers in a cabin-house to the rear of the uppermost deck, as well as in cabins on the deck below.

He left his room to seek some fresh air and found that the crew had just finished cleaning the deck. Despite having an iron hull, ships of this period still had wooden decks and these were traditionally scrubbed every morning. Sailors got down on their hands and knees and scoured the deck with sanding stones and water. This duty was not only, in part, a carryover from the traditions of the Royal Navy, where a daily routine and pride in the ship was expected to encourage discipline amongst the crew, but also a reflection that on-board cleanliness was believed to reduce the risk of disease at sea.

The skies had clouded over, so Neville sought out the pleasantly-furnished saloon which was a kind of on-board living room where passengers could gather. He was the only passenger who had risen, so he sat alone on a sofa and read for a while.

When the ship entered the dreaded Bay of Biscay, the passengers noticed a markedly increased motion of the vessel as it began to be exposed to the forces of the Atlantic Ocean. Neville found that his table in the saloon moved around so much that he could write only with difficulty. Fortunately, the serving of breakfast proved a welcome distraction, and Neville joined the rest of the passengers to eat. He met the captain for the first time – a Scotsman, Andrew McIntosh – who sat at the head of the large table that the passengers shared together, and Neville was again asked to say grace.

There were around 40 passengers on the *Armenian*. During his meal, Neville chatted to a native of Sierra Leone – one of six black Africans on board – an elderly man with white hair whom he refers to as 'Mr N', and he explained to Neville something of the local customs. The other passengers included a ship's captain, two naval men and a major from the army.

The rest of the day was cloudy, cold and gloomy, with occasional rain showers, and the motion of the ship became much more pronounced. Six passengers became so seasick they could not leave their cabins. Neville watched the wind-blown sea, and described it in his diary: 'The colour of the sea is neither green nor blue, but of a pale black, reflecting the hue of the clouds; crests and long streaks of foam of a snowy whiteness everywhere presenting themselves to the eye'.

Overnight the weather deteriorated further. During this era, passengers' beds were bunk-like, and preventer boards were wedged into the sides to prevent sleepers falling out in rough weather, or straps might be provided so that passengers could tie themselves into their beds. High winds and rough seas strained the ship and by early morning a symphony of ship sounds presented themselves to Neville's ears:

'The wind and sea rose, and the ship rocked, rolled, pitched, mounted, and trembled a good deal; then there was the noise of the strain on the ship's timbers, to say nothing of that of the sails, masts, and rigging. These noises, however, I have no objection to, I rather like them, but the incessant hammering noise of the screw-propeller is as though we had a Staffordshire forge in the saloon.'

The noise of a ship at sea was something that all passengers had to get used to, as well as the unfamiliar motion. In the period that Neville was travelling, passenger accommodation was sited to the rear of the ship as this was seen to be the most prestigious location. Anyone who has visited HMS *Victory* will know that Nelson's cabin was in the stern of the ship, and tradition tended to perpetuate the idea that passengers, like senior officers, should have the stern-most quarters furthest away from the bows and the oncoming waves.

In the early days of travel, important passengers were even given the captain's own cabin, as Henry Fielding found on his voyage. However, the problem with having accommodation towards the rear of the ship in the steam era was that it placed passengers closer to the propeller, so it was noisier. It should also be borne in mind that the *Armenian* was small and would only have had two decks, so wherever the cabins were located they would not have been far from the loud, clunking engine room.

Neville battled his way through the ship to enjoy his first meal of the day. Needless to say, breakfast was a challenge in the rough conditions, and the saloon had to be divided into compartments with temporary screens to stop passengers and objects being thrown the length of the room. And, of course, stormy weather at sea was not particularly conducive to eating and some of the passengers who turned up for breakfast had to leave suddenly to return to their cabins.

During the day, Neville did his best to occupy himself. He managed to chat to fellow passengers about his missionary role, and the native man, Mr N, expressed some doubts about his likelihood of success in converting many local adults to Christianity. In particular, he drew attention to the natives' preference for nakedness rather than being clothed, a dislike of monogamy, and an unfamiliarity with money which made them prefer to barter. This rendered Sierra Leone a very different society to Britain, he warned. Neville also spent a lot of time on deck, despite a cold wind, and enjoyed observing wildlife, including a whale, a storm petrel and a school of porpoises that accompanied the ship for some distance.

By Friday, the ocean had settled into what Captain McIntosh called 'a very respectable sea', and the *Armenian* was making ten or eleven knots. Gradually the air began to feel warmer as they headed further and further south. Neville sat on deck near the ship's wheel and watched the 'wide and lofty sea' break over the ship as they continued their good run.

One afternoon, the chief officer decided to open the portholes in Neville's cabin to allow fresh air to circulate, but with the unfortunate result that the sea rushed in and deluged his room, soaking his clothes, his bed and his possessions.

However, this accident was more than made up for the following day, Sunday, when Neville was permitted to conduct divine service on board for both crew and passengers. In his account, he had expressed surprise, on more than one occasion, that during the week he had never been called upon to say evening prayers with the passengers. This was not usual practice on a ship but he had been disconcerted all the same. Surely everyone prayed each evening? Yet it fitted with his preconception that people at sea could sink morally into 'unpleasantness' and 'breaches of decorum' when away from the civilising influences of the rest of society. By this, he was probably concerned

Depiction of a whale from the early 1600s. Thomas Dallam, like many later passengers, enjoyed watching these 'great fishes'.

John Ovington's ship narrowly escaped being drawn into a water spout off the west coast of Africa.

The Pilgrim Fathers bidding farewell to England before embarking on *Mayflower*. Not all the passengers were religious dissenters, but the majority were.

The *Mayflower* passengers passed through Southampton's West Gate in 1620 to board their ship.

A replica of the *Mayflower* at Plimoth Plantation in Massachusetts made using 17th century techniques and materials. It repeated the famous voyage of the original in 1957.

John Ovington took the ship *Benjamin* to Surat in India in 1689 and managed to find refuge in the town's protective harbour just as the monsoon season arrived in late May. However, once the monsoon began to recede, the hot and humid conditions here encouraged infections such as malaria amongst the passengers and most of them died.

An eighteenth century sketch of Henry Fielding in the year that he died. He was only 48 years old, but had been plagued with ill-health and so looks older.

The rock-like, tasteless, and barely nutritious ships' biscuits or 'hard tack' – the basic unappetising rations for passengers and crew alike well into the nineteenth century. Although often full of weevils they kept well on long voyages.

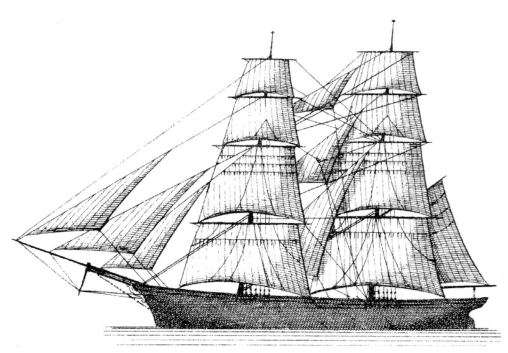

A small eighteenth century brig of the same type as the *Jamaica Packet* that took Janet Schaw to the Caribbean.

The quarterdeck on a Royal Navy ship in about 1820, the era in which Maria Graham travelled as a passenger on board HMS *Doris*.

HMS *Doris* was a typical Royal Navy frigate, and was fast yet heavily armoured.

The *Great Western*, launched in 1838, the first steamship designed for ocean crossing. Note the paddlewheels for propulsion, and that it still carries sails which persisted on steamships until the 1880s.

A burial at sea on an early Victorian passenger ship. The body is on a plank draped in the Union Jack, while the captain reads the Bible, cap removed respectfully. William Smith watched this spectacle with horror in 1847.

One portrayal of the Crossing the Line ceremony in which many passengers have taken part over the centuries.

The typically cramped conditions for emigrants below decks on an 1840s sailing ship like the *India* could encourage the spread of disease. Note the cargo (left) and trunks of passenger belongings (right), which could be dangerous if they broke free in a storm as William Smith discovered.

Mealtime amongst the bunks below decks on an 1840s emigrant ship; the rations were very meagre and monotonously the same day after day. There are ship's biscuits in the tub on the table.

This ship looks like a sailing vessel, but it also has a funnel emitting smoke. It is a barque fitted with a steam engine and a propeller – a "screw barque" – similar to the SS *Armenian* that William Latimer Neville took to Sierra Leone in 1851.

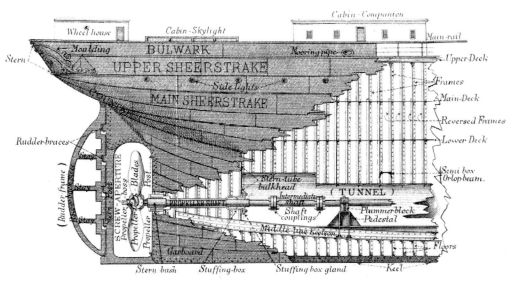

In early steamships, such as the *Armenian*, the vessel's propeller was located just below the main passenger cabins which could be very noisy for passengers, as Neville found out.

Leading officers of SS *London* – first mate Robert Harris and second mate Arthur Ticehurst (standing) did not help passenger John Munro to batten down the hatches; Captain John Martin (seated) told passengers to give up hope of survival. All three went down with the ship.

John King, the seaman from SS *London* that John Munro credited as instrumental in saving his life when the vessel went down. He helped launch the ship's cutter and steered it to safety with nineteen people on board.

*The foundering of the S.S. "LONDON" in the Bay of Biscay, Jan. 11. 1866.*

Contemporary portrayal of the demise of SS *London* in 1866. The sails are torn to shreds, and the engine room flooded. John Munro's escape in the ship's cutter is just visible off the vessel's stern.

A clipper in 1868, the year Mary Perston took one to New Zealand. Slim and streamlined, they were the fastest sailing ships afloat and in favourable conditions could outrun a steamship for short periods.

Arriving in a new world. Many sectors of society emigrated to New Zealand, from the poorest in steerage to the middle classes such as Mary Perston.

Herbert Watts watched the stewards sing and clown around dressed as black men in a so-called 'Christy Minstrels' show for passengers – a common feature of long P&O cruises.

This contemporary sketch shows a cabin on a P&O jubilee steamer such as the SS *Victoria* that carried Herbert Watts to Australia. Note the bunks, and washstand with tap.

Dining on P&O's SS *Victoria* in the late 1880s: a series of long tables where everyone sat together.

P&O's steamship *Victoria* docked at an Australian port where passengers wait to disembark and meet friends and relatives.

Cunard's RMS *Lucania* on which Hubert Whitmarsh travelled to New York in steerage in 1896.

Seasickness – the scourge of passenger travel at sea since it began. Not everyone is affected, but it is more common at the beginning of a voyage until the passenger finds his or her 'sea legs', and when the weather is rough.

Luxury dining for passengers – part of the elegant and imposing dining saloon on *Lusitania*.

A tasteful en suite cabin on *Lusitania*, looking remarkably unlike accommodation on board a ship. The beds are not bunks and are similar to those used ashore with headboards and mattresses. There is a sofa, dressing table, writing desk, and plentiful electric lighting.

Sinking of the Lusitania

Sighting the Submarine

Passengers on the *Lusitania*'s deck sight the German u-boat which sank the liner in 1915 with great loss of life.

Relaxing on the decks of the *Empress* during a world cruise in 1926 as Mr and Mrs Jeffrey did once the ship had left the cold seas of the North Atlantic.

The ever-popular fancy dress ball has been a feature of long-distance cruises since at least the 1880s. This one is amongst second class passengers in 1922.

A page from Mr and Mrs Hunt's honeymoon photo album, showing their Dutch ship *Pieter Corneliszoon Hooft* docked at Algiers with a pontoon alongside to aid disembarkation, and then a picture of both Jane Hunt and her husband James on board.

Jean Davies's photo of the *Boschfontein* looking sternwards in 1937. As can be seen, it was not a luxury liner, being principally a cargo ship that carried passengers. The second picture is of her little friend Gillian; keeping small children entertained on long cruises has never been easy.

Practising in case of disaster – Jean Davies watched the crew's boat drill where they rehearsed the launching of lifeboats.

Reading on deck or sleeping in the sun – two popular passenger pursuits since the earliest days of travel by sea.

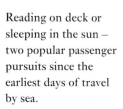

that passengers would engage in shipboard romances, gambling or excessive drinking. He even seems to have been warned that some clergymen could be treated disrespectfully by their fellow passengers – no doubt when voicing objections to the aforementioned behaviour. It is an interesting reflection of the Victorian guardedness against moral deterioration: Neville was so sure that he would encounter this, yet he mentions several times his pleasant surprise at not finding any evidence of it.

But Sunday was Neville's chance to put all this right, as well as to shore up his own religious convictions while away from the fellowship of a church community. Captain McIntosh asked him to lead divine service on the main deck. Accordingly, a group of seamen rigged up an awning overhead to protect the crew and passengers from the glare of the sun, and the capstan was theatrically draped with a union jack. Neville said prayers, led the singing and preached an extempore sermon with a nautical theme. 'With the deep blue Atlantic all around us,' he says, 'it was a solemn and affecting time for me'.

## Sighting Africa

Later on Sunday, the *Armenian* pulled into Funchal Bay, Madeira, a small island off the northwest coast of Africa. A gun was fired to announce their arrival, and shortly afterwards Neville was delighted to discover that an old friend had been rowed out to meet him. His friend insisted Neville stay the night ashore with him, which he gladly accepted. During his visit he tasted 'a delicious tropical fruit' – evidently for the first time. It was called a banana.

After leaving Madeira, the weather deteriorated once more as the ship neared the Canary Islands, with strong winds causing high seas and a rolling and trembling of the ship. So it was with some relief that *Armenian* soon came to anchor in the Bay of Tenerife on Tuesday, 31 August. Neville and four other passengers made up a party that ventured ashore to explore the island.

Returning to the ship for eight o'clock in the evening they continued their voyage southwards. The next morning the sky was blue and clear of cloud, the air soft and warm. The temperatures gradually begin to pick up as they neared the Saharan coast of Africa. The tropical waters attracted large numbers of flying fish which Neville delighted to observe. Yet the heat soon began to become oppressive. On 3 September, the hottest night of the voyage coincided with strong seas, with the result that passengers were shut up in their small rooms without being able to open their portholes for fear of being swamped. The resultant stifling conditions were almost unbearable.

At half-past five the next day, Neville had his first glimpse of the African mainland when the ship anchored at St Mary's Island, The Gambia. Neville again had the opportunity to go ashore and explore and was pleasantly surprised by the standards of education in English at a local school. Before they got under way again, some natives came alongside offering to sell him a live crocodile.

The night after this, Neville's meditations were interrupted at about 10 pm by the bedroom steward entering his cabin to secure the portholes, 'for a tornado,' he said, 'is coming on.'

'And soon it began with furious wind, loud thunder, frequent lightning, and a great rain. The thunder and lightning ceased about two o'clock AM, but now at twelve PM it is still raining and the wind is what I should call a strong one. As every opening – the companion, skylights, and portholes – were fast closed, the heat was very great indeed; and no-one perhaps who has not been in the tropics, or in a warm bath of a very high temperature, can form an idea of what perspiration is in these latitudes.'

This was the Victorian age, so no passenger could have dressed in a manner more befitting the heat: there were no shorts, knee-length skirts, short-sleeved tops, T-shirts or bathing suits. In the stifling heat everyone would have been covered up completely from head to toe, and would have had to grin and bear it. It must have been exceedingly uncomfortable.

The ship continued on its way when the storm passed, and shortly afterwards reached Sierra Leone on Thursday, September 9, where they anchored off Freetown. The day they arrived, the quartermaster, Richard May, was found drunk in the hold. The captain fined him and disrated him – reduced him in rank to seaman.

Neville concludes his account of the voyage by relating his first meeting with his predecessor's subordinate, who would henceforth report to Neville: 'This morning early, before eight o'clock, Mr Duport, the original companion of the martyr Leacock, came on board to welcome me, in the Bishop's name, to Africa'.

After 16 days at sea, the 'great and solemn' adventure in Reverend Neville's life was just about to begin. He found his missionary work very challenging, but after much tribulation he sadly succumbed to a protracted illness, that may have been malaria, after only three years. He, too, had become a martyr like his predecessor.

## Chapter Ten

# A Tragic Storm in the Bay of Biscay

## *(1866, John Munro, SS London)*

John Munro was a Scot, who at the age of around 30 settled in Ballarat, Australia, as a gold miner. However, he had good knowledge of ships because he had been a sailmaker and rigger, and went to sea in this capacity for five-and-a-half years before emigrating. He had been shipwrecked before as a young man, and been trapped in Central America for months trying to secure a passage home. In 1865, aged 36, he came home to Scotland to visit his family, and as the year came to a close, he sought to return to Australia.

The ship that Munro chose in late December 1865 was the SS *London*. She was virtually a new ship, having been launched in 1864, and was owned by Money Wigram and Sons, a company with a perfect safety record, having lost no passenger ships since the company's first voyages in 1847. The *London*, which was around 270 feet long with an iron hull and three masts, was in a different class to many contemporary vessels, being fitted out in luxury to improve the passenger experience on long voyages.

All passenger ships at this time transported significant amounts of cargo: ship owners packed as much on board as they could to increase the profits from a voyage, and such vessels were frequently accused of being 'overladen'. For example, the *London*'s cargo was valued at more than £125,000, whereas the ship itself was only worth £80,000, and the passengers' fares generated perhaps £4,000 at most. The *London*'s large load in 1865 included dead weight such as iron and stone blocks, hardware and tools, and light goods such as textiles, china and medicines. The *London* also carried 500 tons of coal for fuel; the bulky commercial cargo meant that several tons of coal had to be stored on the main deck in sacks.

Built for the run to Australia, the *London* was a fast ship, having made its previous outward voyage in just 59 days, while a sailing ship commonly took three-and-a-half months. The vessel was driven by a single propeller and had a top speed of about nine knots.

The ship had a crew of around 80, including seamen, officers, engine room personnel, canteen staff and stewards. A relative novelty at the time, there was also a female crew member: Grace Logan was a stewardess who tended to the needs of female passengers and children.

The *London*'s captain was John Bohun Martin, an experienced mariner, and known to be very attentive to his passengers. Exact numbers differ between sources, but there were about 160 passengers on board – around 60 in first class, 50 in second class and 50 in third class. John Munro travelled second class, which meant he shared his sleeping area with other passengers rather than having his own cabin, and he also received a more restricted menu at mealtimes.

As has become well known because of later disasters such as the *Titanic*, ships were not required to carry enough lifeboats to rescue everyone on board. The same was true of the *London* but it did have one more boat than the legal minimum – namely seven boats instead of six.

## An Inauspicious Start

The *London* departed from East India Docks on 28 December 1865, bound for Melbourne, but when the vessel anchored at Gravesend the next day, six of her crew deserted. On 30 December, the *London* entered the English Channel guided by a pilot, but the night was wild and a strong wind blew, so the ship lay-to overnight, under the protection of the Isle of Wight.

In peacetime, bad weather was the commonest reason for a ship foundering, so wise captains never took risks. The extent of ship losses during the mid-Victorian era is quite shocking: for the period 1867–1871 a staggering 2,598 ships were lost and 8,807 passengers and crew died. Put another way, this is the loss of an average of ten ships every week at the expense of 34 lives. And yet, alarmingly, these figures only relate to the *coast* of Britain – they say nothing about the many British vessels lost in the Atlantic, Pacific, North Sea and so forth, for which there are no official figures.

Meanwhile, the *London* endured the overnight gale and the next day, despite heavy seas, made it past the Needles and into the open Channel.

However, another gale arose as the vessel steamed westwards: the ship rolled and the passage was uncomfortable, so Munro and the other passengers were confined to their cabins. On 4 January, Captain Martin put into Plymouth to pick up some remaining passengers and decided to stay there to escape the worst of the weather.

A sad incident occurred upon their arrival at Plymouth. A pilot and his assistant put off in a small boat to navigate the *London* to a safe docking, but passengers and crew watched helplessly as a wave capsized their boat when they neared the steamship and threw both men into the water. Despite quickly launching a lifeboat, Captain Martin could only save the pilot's assistant.

At Plymouth, the ship recruited new crewmen to replace the deserters. Some observers here later recalled that the *London* sat rather low in the water – perhaps because of her heavy cargo – but this may simply have been said with the benefit of hindsight.

On 6 January the *London* set sail once more. John Munro noted fine weather, but by the next day there was heavy wind and rain on entering the Bay of Biscay, so only a few sails could be set. Despite the motion of the ship, Munro attended divine service organised by one of the three clergymen on board, but he noticed two problems on deck. The first was that coal stored in sacks on the deck was breaking loose and rolling all over the place, and the second was that the heavy seas were pouring down the hatchways onto the deck below. The hatchways leaked heavily even when they were closed. The crew made no attempt to address either issue.

## A Fearful Storm

The storm continued, and by 8 January many of the passengers were becoming alarmed: 'Some heavy seas came down the main hatchway. Soon after tea, we all turned to and carried the water in buckets up the ladders. Nearly all night the ladies were much frightened'. Munro sat up talking to the female passengers in second class throughout the night, to try and reassure them.

Despite having to enlist the passengers' help to bail out below decks, nothing had been done to prevent the sea cascading down there in the first place: the hatches were not battened down securely. The passengers had a sleepless night as the raging wind and rolling sea noisily buffeted their ship. On 9 January the gale intensified, with the wind strength progressively increasing as the day wore on. The *London*'s heavy cargo encouraged the vessel to plough into, rather than upon, the waves, thus shipping heavy seas and making damage more likely. Munro witnessed this himself: 'At about 10 am lost flying jib-boom, standing jib-boom and foretopmast, carrying all the upper gear with them, together with the main royal mast'.

Munro was appalled that Captain Martin allowed this wreckage to clatter about the decks, along with the loose coal and other debris. This made the main deck a dangerous place to move about on, and the coal was blocking the scuppers that drained water off the ship. The sea also claimed the port-quarter lifeboat as well, lifting it off its davits and carrying it away.

Munro approached the first mate, Robert Harris, with the idea of nailing some tarpaulins over the hatchways to stop water flooding the ship but he wouldn't listen. The second mate, Arthur Ticehurst, gave him a tarpaulin, a hammer and some nails but sent no-one to help him. Munro tried to do it himself but he couldn't do the job alone because the ship was rolling too heavily, so he abandoned the job in despair.

The captain had by this time taken in all sail and was relying upon the engines to give them headway. Yet, by 3 am the next morning, 10 January, their situation still appeared desperate and Captain Martin decided to return to Plymouth. This is a decision for which he was later much criticised. Whilst the captain may have argued that he needed to seek refuge, many commentators felt that he should either have continued in his original direction to run through the storm, or have hoved-to to 'sit it out snugly' like a cork. In turning the ship around, he probably headed back into the worst of the storm.

And so it proved, for the storm intensified again and became exceedingly violent. The minimal sails that had been set were ripped from the ship and went flying away into the darkness. The vessel rolled and pitched, shipping large amounts of water. Another lifeboat was lost along with the ship's cutter, leaving only four boats on board in case they needed to abandon ship. But worse was to come.

The engine room with its coal-stoked fires was located immediately below a skylight on the main deck. The skylight was a frame fitted with sheets of half-inch thick glass; it was over 12 feet by eight feet and weighed a ton-and-a-half. At around 11 am, Munro was in the saloon when he heard the sudden roar of a great body of water flooding into the ship; he raced out and immediately saw the engineers and stokers rushing away from the engine room.

A mountain of water had reared up amidships and come crashing down on the skylight, smashing the glass and tearing the skylight off. This effectively left a large hole immediately over the engine room and as each successive wave broke over the ship, the engine room began to fill with water. The crew tried desperately to nail tarpaulins and sails over the hole, but their efforts were in vain. In no time at all the water level in the engine room was high enough to dowse the fires. No fires meant no engines, so the *London* had no steam power, and sails couldn't be set because of the ferocity of the storm. The ship was thus left without a means of propulsion and at the mercy of the violent wind and waves.

Passengers did what they could with the ship's pumps, and bailed out flooded areas with buckets to try and clear some of the water below decks, and they kept at it all day and through the night. With disgust, Munro realised that only the passengers were manning the pumps. He went below to try and secure help from the seamen but only two would accompany him. The crew were more vigorous when attempting to cover the engine room hatch with tarpaulin or sails to keep the water out, and Munro assisted them, but it made little difference.

By 11 January it was being brought home to many that their situation was verging on the hopeless. Yet early in the morning, a new disaster added to their woes. The inability to keep the ship's bows into the waves meant that the *London* kept slewing around, with the result that waves could crash into her stern, and on one such occasion the vessel's rearmost windows were smashed in. This now allowed water to enter from the stern as well as amidships via the engine room. The carpenter tried to repair the damage but in vain.

Some passengers, fearing the worst, wrote letters to their loved ones and sealed them into bottles which they cast over the side. At least six of these were later found.

Meanwhile, others had not yet given up hope and Munro, for example, was particularly active at the pumps. He found two or three ladies urging the other passengers to work to save the ship as best they could. He particularly noticed a Mrs Chapman:

'She was going about the saloon trying to get volunteers for the pumps, and encouraging all about her to work. I had just come in from a spell at the pumps, when I met her. She asked me to go. She said, cheeringly – "Come, you're a strong man, go and work". I told her I had been working for some time, and was tired. She answered that I, "ought not to be tired at such a time". I went again, well knowing that it was of little or no use; but I could not help going when she asked me. She pressed many more to go, and I never saw or heard one refuse her.'

Amidst these frantic attempts to save the ship, those on deck were constantly assaulted by breaking waves and debris thrown about them. Captain Martin clearly thought the whole situation beyond hope, yet some crewmen began launching the ship's boats without assistance from their officers. With only four boats left, Munro worked with seaman John King and others to prepare the iron-hulled pinnace which could hold 50. In their haste, it was lowered too quickly, filled with water and sank like a stone. Munro, King and others were on board when the pinnace sank beneath their feet but they all somehow scrambled back onto the *London*.

## Abandoning Ship

Having seen the fate of the first boat, the crew were disinclined to launch a second, but their ship was sinking fast, so they attempted to lower the portside cutter. Munro and King again assisted, and this time they were successful, but they had great difficulty persuading any passengers to join them. Most had now gathered in the first class saloon and were being encouraged to pray and prepare to meet their end by the three clergymen on board. The passengers were also aware that the pinnace had simply sunk, and consequently held no expectation of survival in the much smaller cutter. Indeed, Captain Martin himself was so convinced there was no hope for anyone on board, that he had addressed all the passengers in the saloon and told them so.

A lady passenger later confided to the captain that she wanted to join Munro in the cutter: 'Mrs Owen expressed a wish to go but the captain advised her not to attempt it, as, in his opinion, there was no chance for the boat, and her sufferings would only be protracted'.

Munro and others remarked upon the curious mental state of the passengers, who seemed wholly resigned to their fate. No stampeding to the boats, no hysterics or violence. Religious commentators at the time attributed this to the hard work of the clergymen, preparing the passengers to meet their maker bravely. The ministers had been busy praying, counselling and preaching for almost two days. But perhaps it was the obvious despair of the ship's officers and a simple lack of belief that anyone could survive in the face of such a ferocious storm that ultimately made most people on board abandon themselves to their fate. The men felt that their wives or children could not possibly endure time in an open boat at sea, so decided to stay with them until the end.

Yet Munro was a determined man. With just a single space left in the cutter, he went back to try and save one more passenger. He spotted his friend from Ballarat, Mr Hickman, with his wife and four children. Even the saloon was filling with water now, and time was short:

'It was impossible that the poor children could escape: not one of them could be expected to take the fearful leap required: nor could Mrs Hickman; but her husband – he could escape, perhaps, if he would, and if the boat did live out the fearful sea, he might be saved.'

Munro urged his friend to consider it but he, of course, refused. How could he contemplate abandoning his family? Munro helped Hickman's children to a drier spot, they shook hands, said their farewells and Munro departed. He persuaded a young woman to come with him, but when she saw the distance she would have to jump over the ship's side to reach the boat she couldn't bring herself to do it. She would have had to leap from the *London* into the raging seas in order to be picked up – not an attractive prospect. As he pleaded with her, Munro's hand was caught as the boat jarred against the side of the *London*, squeezing a stone from a ring he wore.

In the end, it was another crewman who decided to join them in the cutter, not a passenger – John Jones, one of the engineers. Thus the cutter left the *London*'s side with 19 men on board: 16 crewmen and just three male passengers – John Munro, David Main and Edward Wilson. This was seven more than the boat was built to carry. Mrs Chapman kindly threw them a blanket and a parcel of herrings, having already provided blankets from her cabin. Captain Martin tossed his compass down, gave them a course, and wished them luck. The boat left the ship's side at about 2pm: 'As the boat got a little distance off, I saw Mrs Chapman wave a white handkerchief. Some waved their caps, and others their handkerchiefs, and some cheered'.

Munro felt that Mrs Chapman encouraged their departure so that someone might get back home and let the passengers' families know their fate; she herself could not abandon ship as she was travelling with young children. Even so, at least one person realised, too late, that he had a better chance of survival with Munro and colleagues. A young man, the doctor's assistant on board, rushed to the rail and offered the cutter's occupants £500 if they would come back for him: 'But at that time the boat was too far off: had it been the King of England, we could not have taken him in, the wind and sea were so high at the time, and the ship was in a sinking state'.

Within a few short minutes, it was all over for the *London*:

> 'I am sure that not more than five minutes had elapsed after the boat had shoved off from the ship's side when we lost sight of the London. Not a vestige of her was to be seen on the top of the waves. All in the boat saw her go down. We were not more than eighty or ninety yards from her when we saw her stem rise high out of the water, so as to expose forty or fifty feet of her keel forwards; of course her stern must have then sunk under water. The boat then fell into the trough of the sea, and when we rose to the crest of the waves, the London had disappeared.'

Members of the *London*'s crew had been trying to prepare two other boats for launch, but it was all too late now.

The survivors in the cutter pulled away from the wreck site as best they could; John King had to steer the boat with a length of driftwood, and they shipped a great deal of water as the storm continued. After three hours they sighted a ship but being winter, it was already getting dark, so they were difficult to spot. They spied another vessel at 4 am but although their hails were returned, this second ship could not find them in the darkness. Finally, after 20 hours at sea in an open boat without fresh water, they sighted two other ships at 10 am, and decided to make for the one to starboard:

'We manned the oars and pulled lustily for about an hour and a half, when we came alongside of the Italian barque Marianople of Genoa, bound from Constantinople to Cork or Falmouth for orders. We had some difficulty in getting on board, but at length, with the assistance of those belonging to the barque, we all got safely on board, about noon, on Friday the 12th of January. We were very kindly treated, and landed at Falmouth on the following Tuesday.'

The precise death toll on the *London* is difficult to ascertain because figures differ between sources. However, around 220 passengers and crew were lost, and only the 19 saved. Munro was critical of the officers on board the *London* whom, he felt, accepted their fate without a struggle and 'not one of the officers made any attempt to save himself or the ship'. However, he gives unreserved praise to John King, without whom Munro and the others on the cutter might not have survived: 'In fact it was John King, an able seaman, who took command, and who had greatly contributed to getting the boat safely away from the ship. He showed a great deal of skill in dodging the heavy seas as they broke, and in laying the boat alongside of the barque'.

On his eventual return to Ballarat in April 1866, the town held a dinner in John Munro's honour to welcome him home. He led a long life as a gold miner, and died in 1920 at the grand old age of 92 – the last survivor of the SS *London*. By coincidence, John King, the seaman instrumental in his survival, also moved to Australia and their shared experience meant they kept in touch throughout their lives.

## Chapter Eleven

# Emigration to New Zealand by Clipper

## *(1868, Mary Perston, Coleroon)*

Mary Eliza Perston was born in Scotland but had been brought up on the Isle of Man where her father was a magistrate. At 24 years of age she decided to emigrate to New Zealand to join her brother Willie. She knew the voyage would be long but booked the speedy clipper *Coleroon* for her passage.

Miss Perston's account is interesting because it marks the beginning of the end for long distance passenger travel by clipper ship. Once the Suez Canal opened the following year, in 1869, it was quicker and more comfortable to take a steamship to Australia or New Zealand.

In 1868, ships bound for New Zealand pursued the long route around the Cape of Good Hope. Some steamships undertook this route in the 1860s – in the previous chapter it was noted that the ill-fated SS *London* reached Australia in only 59 days in 1865 – but clipper ships were widely used because they were cheaper to run. Yet after Suez opened, sailing ships for passengers to Australasia started to become less common. By the 1880s, a steamship could reach Australia in around a month, as described in the next chapter.

### The Only Passenger

The *Coleroon* was a familiar ship on the Australia and New Zealand run. Mary Perston joined the vessel at London on 25 March.

Her first impressions were, in her own words, 'rather miserable' as there were no other passengers aboard and the ship was a mess. Passenger accommodations had yet to be prepared, while seamen, carpenters, riggers and sailmakers were labouring to ensure *Coleroon* was seaworthy. A large assorted cargo was being lowered into the hold or was waiting on deck to be stowed by the crew. Food and water were being loaded too: dried provisions, and fresh ones such as vegetables, plus live chickens and sheep to feed the passengers. The ship was also transporting three cows for a New Zealand farmer. So it was a noisy and untidy time – and a little disheartening to an inexperienced young traveller.

The steward, Arthur Blake, apologised that Miss Perston's tea was simply boiled meat slapped on a plate but explained that meals would be better once at sea. After a few hours watching all that was going on, Miss Perston went to bed in her cabin and slept remarkably well.

Early next morning, the *Coleroon* started down the Thames and by half past five had reached Gravesend where the rest of the passengers joined them. Four travellers joined Miss Perston in first class: Mr Troupe, Mr Bentley, Mr Smith and Miss Rathbone. Clipper ships had limited space, so Miss Perston shared her cabin with Miss Rathbone but, having arrived first, secured the lower of the two bunks for herself which was more comfortable. There were 17 passengers in second class, and 11 travelling third class (which was becoming a more polite term for 'steerage') including one child.

Miss Perston was delighted to discover that first class had its own cat and two kittens 'to keep away the rats'. Rodents were a nuisance: they ate food or cargo and were liable to damage the vessel itself by gnawing. Consequently most Victorian ships carried at least one cat. Besides catching rats, the ship's cat offered companionship to those on board and was also considered lucky.

That night, Miss Perston didn't sleep well; she was kept awake by the officer of the watch pacing the deck above her head: 'There was such a 'tramp, tramp' overhead all night. Mr Bentley proposed offering the man a pair of galoshes [rubber overshoes] if he would wear them, and another proposed to give him five shillings if he would only walk on the other side of the vessel – which Mr Bentley hoped he would not, as it is his side'.

When she did eventually get to sleep she was woken early by the crew scrubbing the decks – 'such a row' – but the first officer, Moses Carden, had to have the vessel clean to welcome the captain, Edward Montgomery, who arrived shortly afterwards to inspect his ship. *Coleroon* was made ready, and left Gravesend at 2.30 pm on 27 March.

## The Voyage Begins

Sharing a small cabin was not easy. Both passengers needed space for their belongings, and there was no privacy. For example, in practice there was not enough room for two women to get dressed at the same time. Nonetheless, once at sea Miss Perston slept better; she heard the seasick Miss Rathbone call out at night, but ignored her because there was little she could do to help. Henceforward, Miss Rathbone confined herself to their cabin for a few days.

'I am left to myself to entertain the gentlemen: we are now all on speaking terms. I am still a wee bit sick but not laid up. I did not appear at the breakfast table as I was afraid of the consequences; I guessed right. I sat down to dinner, but had after all to go without – provoking, as I was hungry – but I took my tea at tea time. I am not minding the motion on deck much. It is delightful but rather cold.'

The *Coleroon* made five to six knots through the English Channel. Miss Perston started to read a recently-published book – Elizabeth Charles's *Diary of Miss Kitty Trevelyan* – a novel about clergymen from the era of John Wesley. But she did some writing herself, too. As well as updating her daily journal, she wrote two letters – to her sister and to her uncle. Passengers often gave letters to the ship's pilot when he departed, and Miss Perston gave him both of hers for posting.

On her first Sunday, she realised with disappointment that there would be no divine service. As noted in previous chapters, unless there happened to be a minister on board, organised worship depended on the religious proclivities of the captain. Captain Montgomery was not inclined to arrange anything, so public worship did not take place.

However, although Miss Rathbone was still seasick, Sunday was the first day that Miss Perston attended every meal. 'We get very nice fare on board,' she wrote, 'and plenty of it'. Her dinner consisted of soup, then a choice of 'fowls, mutton, ham, beef', followed by plum pudding, then cheese – all served by the attentive steward, Blake. Helping the sickly Miss Rathbone to bed made Miss Perston herself queasy, but the captain gave her a little brandy which cured her. The next day the dinner menu was soup, fresh mackerel, roast beef, boiled mutton and cherry tart. Captain Montgomery stopped a Cornish fishing vessel to barter for the mackerel – swapping eight sticks of tobacco and a bottle of rum for the fish.

Long voyages in close confinement can make or break friendships. But after three days afloat, Miss Perston had already become tired of her doleful roommate with her constant illness: 'Miss Rathbone is still very ill. I do not know what she will do if rough weather comes on… I like the Miss Taylors, what I have seen of them. Miss Rathbone is from Birmingham: I do not think much of her'.

The Taylors were in second class: father, mother, aunt, two adult daughters and a son. They were travelling to New Zealand to perform as a family choir. Apart from being constantly ill, Miss Rathbone soon revealed herself in Miss Perston's eyes as 'stupid', disorganised and ill-prepared for travel. By the end of the voyage the two roommates barely spoke.

## Passing Time

When *Coleroon* entered the Bay of Biscay it began rolling, which Miss Perston found very disconcerting. Yet as they became accustomed to the ship's motion and each other, the passengers grew more creative at organising their own entertainment: 'Mr Troupe and Mr Bentley went up the rigging for fun. The sailors made Mr Troupe fast – tied him to the rigging. Mr Bentley, seeing the fate of Mr Troupe, slid down a rope in double-quick time. We had a game of whist tonight: Mr Smith and I against Mr Troupe and Miss Rathbone. Each had a game'.

Miss Perston's quickly-established daily routine included whist in the evenings followed by a walk on deck if the weather permitted. Intrigued by her fellow travellers, Miss Perston was allowed to see the ship's passenger list. Modern genealogists know these often contain inaccuracies and she verified this: 'All our ages are marked down in a list the captain has. Miss Rathbone is put down 20; she is 24 in September. I was put down 28 – just fancy: four years more than it ought to have been!'

The first week sped by. Despite the trials of her roommate, Miss Perston enjoyed the company of her fellow passengers and her time on deck with the fresh air, views and sunsets. She soon found that she could sleep through the early morning noise of the decks being scrubbed, and although she wasn't fond of Miss Rathbone, she still managed to coax her on deck to improve her health.

The passengers sought to entertain themselves and there was a proposal to put on a theatrical performance and to publish a shipboard newspaper. A few issues of the paper were produced but it, like the theatre, came to nothing because not enough people were interested. One day the men in first class took to throwing bottles overboard and firing at them with a pistol. However, card games remained popular, often playing for pennies, and even the captain joined in some evenings: '2 April. Played vingt-et-un [pontoon] at a penny per dozen. I neither lost nor won as I was banker. I did very well. The extent lost was four-and-a-half pence by the captain. We played two hours. We are glad to have it to do as it helps to keep us from thinking of the rolling'.

The ship's rolling often stopped Miss Perston from taking her daily walks, although Mr Bentley accompanied her sometimes to stop her falling. A strong wind with a sea swell made the vessel roll, but it also meant a faster passage: a constant 7 knots enabled a sailing vessel to travel around 170 nautical miles per day. Conversely, a gentle wind was more comfortable for passengers but progress was slow. For example, by the second Sunday, the wind had eased but *Coleroon* could only make 3 knots and so travelled a mere 80 miles in 24 hours. On Monday progress was even worse – just 40 miles.

Nonetheless Miss Perston was still enjoying herself and the time passed quickly. As many passengers have found since, life on board became structured around eating: 'I like the life on board now. It is very lazy, certainly. The meal hours seem all to come very quickly. Breakfast is half-past eight; lunch twelve o'clock; dinner half-past two; tea six o'clock; biscuits and grog is eight. It just seems [as if I am] eating all day'.

The regularity of meals helped Miss Perston understand timekeeping on British ships. The ship's bell was rung day and night according to a pattern of 'watch' periods when an officer or senior crewman took charge of the main deck. The watches were:

| Afternoon watch | Noon to 4 pm |
| Afternoon watch | Noon to 4 pm |
| First dogwatch | 4 pm to 6 pm |
| Second dogwatch | 6 pm to 8 pm |
| First watch | 8 pm to midnight |
| Middle or mid watch | Midnight to 4 am |
| Morning watch | 4 am to 8 am |
| Forenoon watch | 8 am to noon |

The bell was rung once after the first 30 minutes of each watch, then twice after one hour, three times after an hour-and-a-half, and so on until 'eight bells' which indicated the end of a four hour watch. Passengers quickly learned to translate this into 'shore' time.

Despite her overall enjoyment of the voyage, most of the other passengers were a disappointment to Miss Perston. Earlier favourable impressions of the Miss Taylors in second class, for instance, quickly soured: 'The second class are always making some fuss about their arrangements. We have no reason to complain: all is as comfortable as possible. I do not care for any of the second class passengers. Except for the captain and the three gentlemen, there is no one worth speaking to'.

## Changes Afloat

On 7 April they passed Lisbon. Miss Perston taught Mr Bentley to play backgammon in the warmth on deck, and she enjoyed a beautiful sunset. The weather had been good so far, and they all had become used to the motion of the ship. Stomachs had settled and there was no more seasickness. But the next morning everything changed quite dramatically, and continued for the next two days:

'8 April: The wind has risen, and now instead of rolling we are at pitch and toss. It is not nearly so pleasant: everybody is feeling the change.

9 April: What a change today – all sick. I managed to get up on deck. It was a little better, but still it was a scene which I cannot describe.

When breakfast time came all wished to eat if possible, but it was not easy. The captain and chief officer, Mr Carden, were the only ones at the table. The steward brought us ours on deck, but no sooner one got something down they had to make for the edge of the vessel – at least the gentlemen did, we [ladies] had to get a basin. I was not very bad compared to the others, and would have been all right if the sea had not washed over the poop, so that we were forced to go below. No one appeared except the captain and Mr Carden for dinner or tea. Most retired to their berths, and made the best of it there. We could not help laughing at each other, sick as we were.'

The weather eventually improved but Miss Perston was left with a day-long headache, probably caused by dehydration. She was also unsteady on her feet and slipped twice when the captain took her for a walk along the wet deck. She generally took an hour's walk most evenings but liked to be accompanied.

Miss Perston visited Captain Montgomery every day to monitor the ship's progress. Their course took them from Portugal and then down the coast of Africa. Her time with the captain was the highlight of her day – although she knew he was a married man – because the daily routine had suddenly become somewhat boring: 'Life on board is getting so monotonous that at times I do not care to sit down and write. I always come down below at twelve o'clock for a biscuit, and it is getting a regular thing now for the captain to give me a glass of sherry. Even although I say 'no', he says I am better for it. It is very kind of him'.

The captain gave her wine too, although the other passengers had to pay for it. She confided to him that she now avoided the second class passengers, and he agreed with her because otherwise, 'a quarrel is so often the result between first and second class passengers'. However, to keep herself busy, the ever-industrious Miss Perston embroidered a blouse when she had no other entertainment.

The climate was becoming warmer as they neared the equator and Miss Perston realised that her hands had become very brown. Bearing in mind it was only mid-April, the temperature in her cabin was 28°C and she decided she needed to bathe. Passengers with cabins could wash in their rooms using a basin of water, but complete immersion was not so straightforward. *Coleroon* had a bath that could be filled with seawater, so Miss Perston rose extra early to avoid being seen, and took a bath. The next day the male passengers had a shower; standing on the forecastle at 6 am, before the ladies came on deck, they were showered with seawater by a crewman using the deck-pump.

By 23 April the temperature in Miss Perston's cabin was a muggy 34°C, the heat exacerbated by several days of very little wind. In the ensuing 24 hours they only made eight miles and 'everybody is complaining of the heat'. The captain lowered a boat for some of the passengers to be rowed across the ocean for a change of scene, and they all enjoyed it tremendously. The heat and the lack of wind continued for an agonising nine days and even the seasoned Captain Montgomery said he would 'get cranky if it lasts much longer'. The build-up of heat led to lightning in the skies most evenings, and sometimes short bursts of rain. Miss Perston wrote a batch of letters in the hope that they would spot a ship to take them back home for her.

**Frustrations and Bad Behaviour**

Persistent calms and winds from the wrong quarter were incredibly vexing. An occasional light wind might blow them along for half an hour but then as quickly disappear again. Casting about for something to occupy herself, Miss Perston offered to mend the ship's signal flags – a pleasant task that took five days to complete. The few vessels they passed were frustratingly too far away to take their letters. On 2 May, the Coleroon crossed the equator and the captain promised they would soon encounter the tradewinds and make better progress. The next day this proved correct.

Three days later, 5 May, opened with a row. The second mate was caught stealing. Physical punishment was not generally administered to crew members in the merchant navy, but financial or legal penalties were common. He had already been cautioned once by Captain Montgomery for drunkenness but this time he had to be punished. He was disrated – reduced in rank from mate to ordinary seaman – and ordered to vacate his officer's cabin and sleep in a hammock like the rest of the seamen. Another crewman, William McTaggart, was promoted in his place.

A major method of controlling bad behaviour amongst seamen was limiting their alcohol intake. Captain Montgomery only issued rum on Saturdays or on special occasions after extra duties. However, Miss Perston noticed drunkenness quite often amongst the crew early in the voyage.

Annoyingly, the tradewinds unexpectedly died away and *Coleroon* was once again left drifting slowly for days on end, almost two weeks in fact. It became so dull that Miss Perston stopped writing her journal for 11 days. She resumed on 22 May:

'I have not written any for some time. Everything had got so very monotonous and the wind has been so variable of late. A squall would come sometimes, and although it sent us below, it sent the ship along so nicely that we did not mind it. Then for days after it was only going a few knots an hour, and everything got so very tame: nothing to do except read and walk, or sitting all day long.'

Eventually, the situation improved, but the resulting more boisterous seas caused other problems. Miss Perston relates tales of soup or condiments leaping off the table and into her lap at mealtimes, and her many tumbles as she passed around the ship:

'This morning I was standing talking to Mr Smith at the door of his cabin, one half of which was open. I leant against the other half, when the ship gave an extra roll and away went the door and I after it, straight into the cabin. I landed under the bed, and there I lay unable to move for laughing and Mr Smith equally helpless.'

Yet despite these mishaps the *Coleroon* cruised at an average of 200 miles per day for the next four days as they raced past the remote island of Tristan da Cunha, but Miss Perston noticed it was colder and went on deck with a shawl. Soon a fire was lit in the lounge to warm the passengers.

As *Coleroon* headed south, the evenings came on sooner as well, and this restricted the time for entertainments such as card games and reading. Passengers were provided with candles according to the class of passage they had booked. First class passengers were given one candle per night, which burned for five hours, providing a feeble cabin light from 5 pm until 10 pm. However, second class were given one candle every two nights and third class were given none. The Taylor family, whom Miss Perston had grown to loathe, complained that they needed more candles, but the captain explained that stocks were limited and that issuing more now would mean insufficient candles later in the voyage. Tensions flared, and Mr Taylor's sister argued with the captain so loudly that everyone else could hear, yet he yielded nothing: 'I never heard *anyone* talk like Miss Taylor does – no-one likes her on board. She is always having some row'.

However, despite these strains, the ship made good progress and on 29 May, the captain informed Miss Perston that the *Coleroon* had passed the Cape of Good Hope and had run 225 miles in the past day – the greatest distance the ship would travel in 24 hours during the entire voyage. This was an average speed of just over 9 knots. In extraordinary circumstances clippers could attain greater speeds than the steamers of their day, but not consistently. In 1854, for example, the appropriately-named *Lightning* once made 436 miles in 24 hours – an average speed of over 18 knots – much faster than any steamship of the period. But daily distances in excess of 300 miles were not routine, and for every fast day there were usually many more slow ones.

Within a few days tensions flared again in second class and there was fighting amongst the passengers that put 'all the Miss Taylors into hysterics'. With a wearisome air, Miss Perston explains that it was not worth even describing the reasons for the fisticuffs, and she continued to avoid those involved. She had learned some new card games and continued to play most evenings with Mr Bentley.

## Lost and Found

Once past the Cape, the *Coleroon* repeatedly ran into gales for the second half of the voyage. The long succession of bad weather kept the passengers cooped up below decks and this was frustrating. A dramatic storm with tremendously heavy rain hit the ship at the end of May. The thunder sounded like 'a cannon had been discharged at your ear' and at night the lightning in the darkness blinded everyone on deck. The next morning everyone was amazed that one passenger, Mr Troupe, had slept through it all. Of more concern, however, was that the prolonged cloudiness thereafter meant that Captain Montgomery could not take a sighting of the sun or stars for days on end, and the *Coleroon* got lost, running miles off course. Eventually, finding their position again, the ship was then met by two storms in June:

'23 June: We have had two severe gales, the first on Sunday was bad, but the one yesterday was worse. The sea rose mountains high, and seemed to be continually smoking. During the first gale we had to 'lay to' for eight hours and yesterday we 'lay to' for ten hours. The ship rolled and pitched so it was all we could do to keep our seats. In fact we all looked the picture of misery: everything was either wet or uncomfortable in some other way … We got no sleep for two nights.'

The rough seas caused large quantities of water to find their way below decks, and many of the passengers' cabins were flooded. The crew spent hours bailing it all out. During one gale, an apprentice seaman called Colson fell from one of the spanker spars to the deck below. He was fortunate that he only sprained his foot, but he could not walk for a long time afterwards.

## Reaching a New Home

On 4 July *Coleroon* passed Tasmania. Although they could not see the island, they all knew their voyage was almost over. However, there was one last drama before the end: the ship's steward, Blake, was caught stealing gin. Miss Perston surmised this was the cause of the drunkenness she had seen earlier in the voyage. When confronted, Blake became disobedient and refused to obey orders, so Captain Montgomery promised to hand him over to the police in New Zealand.

On 8 July at 6 am, the captain knocked on Miss Perston's door to call her on deck. She had wanted to be the first passenger to sight The Snares – a small island group about 125 miles south of New Zealand. It was bitterly cold, and there had been sleet overnight but she saw the dark rocks by moonlight: the first land she had seen since Portland in the English Channel more than 100 days previously.

Three days later the ship nosed towards snow-covered Lyttelton in New Zealand's South Island. On 12 July, a pilot took the *Coleroon* to its anchorage and the following day Miss Perston stepped ashore to send a telegram to brother Willie. At this point she said goodbye to most of the other passengers and went for a long walk with Captain Montgomery. He said it had been a good passage, bearing in mind the ship was heavily laden with cargo.

The next day, *Coleroon* departed for Wellington with 70 new passengers on board. The going was such that almost all of them, including Miss Perston, were violently seasick but eventually the ship reached her final destination of Wellington on 17 July. Miss Perston had been on board the *Coleroon* for 115 days.

She said goodbye to the captain and, disembarking, immediately recognised her brother Willie. Her nephews were excited to see her but Miss Perston was even more pleased to learn that her brother had a new baby and that he and his wife had delayed the baptism so that she could be present.

Mary Perston never married but lived a contented life in New Zealand with her brother's family. The *Coleroon* continued her long distance voyages as a cargo ship until 1873, when sadly the ageing vessel was lost in a storm in the Indian Ocean, taking the captain and all his crew with it.

*Chapter Twelve*

# Steamship to Australia with P&O

## *(1888, Herbert Watts, SS* Victoria*)*

Herbert Watts decided to take a voyage to Adelaide, Australia, to visit friends and relatives. Accompanying him were four friends: Mary Witherby and her half-brother Charlie Burney, whom Watts knew best; Thomas Smith, and the enigmatic Miss Collier whose first name is never revealed. Charlie was 18 years old, but the rest of the party were all in their twenties and were the children of professional people – Watts' father was a solicitor, for instance – and they were travelling first class. Fortunately, Watts left a handwritten account of the voyage.

### First Few Days

Watts boarded the ship at Royal Albert Docks, London, at 11.30 am on Friday, 19 October 1888. His companions were already on board – Herbert Watts had a habit of leaving things until the last minute and they were no doubt keen to avoid waiting around for him at the docks.

Their vessel was the SS *Victoria* owned by the Peninsular and Oriental Steam Navigation Company, more familiarly known as P&O. The *Victoria* was one of four 'jubilee' ships that the company had launched to mark two 50th anniversaries: that of Queen Victoria's accession, and of P&O receiving its first contract to carry the British mail. At the time of Watts sailing on *Victoria*, she was still a very new ship, having taken her maiden voyage only late the previous year. Her three sister ships were the *Britannia*, *Oceana* and *Arcadia*, all launched in 1887–1888 and each of them considerably larger than any previous P&O ship. *Victoria* was a little over 465 feet in length with a maximum width of 52 feet, and a gross tonnage of 6,091.

Watts made his way to his cabin, which he shared with Charlie. 'First class' in 1888 did not mean a capacious and luxuriously appointed cabin.

In Watts' case, it meant a small private room, simply decorated, with two single bunk beds and some storage space for clothes and luggage. There was accommodation on board for 230 first class passengers, and 156 in second class.

There had been many steamship improvements since George Moore's experiences in 1844 (Chapter 7). It is a rather stark generalisation but before the 1880s, a voyage was taken largely through necessity rather than for pleasure, even though it may have had its enjoyable moments. But in Watts' account we witness the growth of ship owners' and crews' attempts to cultivate and entertain passengers. First class cabins, for example, had cold running water which came from a small tank above the washstand that was topped up by an attendant each day, so Watts could shave each morning; passengers could also take hot baths in bathrooms distributed around the ship. An important technological development for passenger comfort came in 1881 when electric lights were introduced on British commercial ships. P&O quickly adopted them on the *Chusan* in 1884, and thereafter all new P&O ships, including the *Victoria*, came with electric lighting as standard.

The *Victoria* was pulled away from its jetty by a tug at 1 pm and into deeper water. Once the voyage began, Watts walked around the decks of the ship for about an hour, to familiarise himself with the basic layout. P&O provided its passengers with a map to assist them. His cabin was on the main deck, roughly amidships, and there were a number of large, sumptuously decorated communal areas to explore – the first class saloon incorporated a large dining room, a music room with a piano, and a smoking room.

Suddenly hungry, Watts ventured into the saloon to enjoy what he and the shipping line liked to call 'tiffin'. This was an experience exclusive to first class on P&O; tiffin was an Anglo–Indian word meaning a light midday meal or lunch. During this era, P&O had a reputation for luxury travel that was second to none amongst British passengers travelling to the Mediterranean, India, south east Asia and Australasia. A major determinant of this status was the high quality of the food served on board. The company had also made a conscious effort to appeal only to the upper end of the travel market and so did not offer cheap third class or 'steerage' accommodation that would be taken up by emigrants. Passengers were first class or second class only, with first class predominating in terms of numbers.

After lunch, the passengers were asked to decide when they wanted their evening meal each day. There were two choices: 6 pm or 7.30 pm, and Watts and his friends chose the latter. It was explained to them that any letters they wrote would be collected from the vessel when they stopped at a port and despatched back home via mail ships, so Watts and Mary went below and wrote a letter to Watts' mother. By about 10.30 on his first night, however, Watts had retired to bed 'as the motion was getting rather too much', yet although he felt a little seasick, he did sleep fairly well.

The next morning, he arose at 8.30 am 'feeling not quite the thing' but made himself go and have breakfast. There was a beautiful view of the Isle of Wight as he strolled back to his cabin and here the *Victoria* halted briefly to allow the pilot who had navigated them thus far, to return to shore. By 11.30, Watts was feeling considerably worse, so he 'went and got a bottle of champagne and retired to my cabin' where he stayed all day. Perhaps unsurprisingly, the next morning he could not stomach the idea of either breakfast or the Sunday service. At lunchtime he was still 'much too ill for even the sight of tiffin', yet he found that not eating did help to settle him and he was able stay on deck and get some fresh air. He made do with sipping some beef tea and nibbling dry biscuits occasionally. Thankfully, by the evening, his symptoms were sufficiently alleviated to restore his appetite and he was able to eat a proper meal of 'roast beef and turkey', and for the first time he had a very good night's sleep.

On Monday, having acquired his sea legs, Watts was at last able to enjoy the voyage. Everything on board was geared around the three main meals of the day, which helped passengers to establish a routine for themselves by providing fixed points that broke the day into manageable chunks. Watts' principal meals were typically: breakfast around 9 am, tiffin at 1 pm, and dinner at 7.30 pm, although he might also take tea and supper as well.

When the weather was good, Watts and his friends spent a lot of their time on deck. So as *Victoria* crossed the Bay of Biscay, the group devoted many hours to enjoying the sunshine and fresh air, and taking in the beautiful view of the coast. The ship provided an array of deck chairs, upright wicker chairs, folding 'picnic' chairs and benches for passengers on which to relax. There were also traditional deck entertainments such as quoits. At half-past four, there was a short concert by the ship's band which lasted about an hour. Watts then retired to dress for dinner before eating at 7.30. At the start of a cruise, passengers usually went to bed well before midnight, and Watts was not atypical in turning in at 10.45.

Watts makes no mention of stowaways in his account, but as ships became larger it was easier for people to sneak on board and hide as cargo was being loaded, or when well-wishers came to bid passengers farewell. These non-paying passengers were commonly discovered near the beginning of a voyage, in which case there was sometimes the opportunity to send them back ashore. Otherwise they might be dropped off at the ship's first port of call, or even arrested, but sympathetic captains would allow them free passage if they worked hard in return. In 1883, for example, William Lilley on a voyage to Australia describes the fate of a stowaway on the SS *Orient*:

'The talk this morning on deck was about the finding of a stowaway. A young fellow looking very much like a London costermonger was found hidden behind the boiler. He was brought out and taken to the captain who, after questioning him, decided that he should be allowed to work his passage out to Sydney… As I went past the engine-room about eight o'clock, I found him working away with a will, cleaning the brass-work, well content with his lot. He told me that he was unmarried and he hoped, after he had worked his passage out, to do better in the new country than in the old. Sometimes as many as nine or ten stowaways have been found on board this ship. Generally these poor fellows have friends among the seamen, and sometimes their presence on board is connived at by the mates of the ship, as in that way they can get an extra hand or two at little cost.'

## Mediterranean and Suez

Returning to the *Victoria*, it was now 23 October and the ship had arrived at Gibraltar. The weather was still glorious and the passengers had the opportunity to step on shore to explore 'the Rock', but Watts, as usual, had not got himself ready and to his dismay he realised that his friends, quicker off the mark, had scrambled into a steam launch with the other passengers and there didn't seem to be any room for him. As the steamer sped away,

Watts cast around for means to get ashore and joined forces with a passenger named Drummond. Between them they caught the attention of a local man with his small boat and he rowed them ashore. Yet Watts' disappointment is palpable when he finds that his friends had not waited for him.

Nevertheless, Watts and Drummond hired a carriage and were driven all around the town, enjoying the sights, a local market and the continued good weather. They returned to the *Victoria* at six o'clock. Interestingly, Drummond does not appear in the list of first class passengers and having found it convenient to associate with him for the purposes of touring Gibraltar, Watts never mentions him again.

Watts continued to structure his day around mealtimes. Each meal was announced by a steward blowing a tune on a bugle. Passengers were expected to dress formally for dinner, but might wear any smart attire for other meals.

In between eating, passengers relaxed in the sunshine, wrote letters and played games. There was also an extensive library on board. Watts kept his journal up to date every day during the voyage. He also regularly participated in a daily sweepstake that the saloon passengers organised between them. Each person had to guess the total number of miles the ship would travel that day, and paid one shilling to enter. The winner who came closest to guessing the real mileage – the ship's 'run' – as verified by the purser would receive all the money. The mileage was posted up every day at noon underneath a map of their route. *Victoria* steamed ahead day and night, and in a complete 24-hour period would typically cover between 300 and 400 miles, but this was affected considerably by the weather – especially wind speed and direction.

During the voyage, Watts got to know the *Victoria*'s second engineer quite well. By coincidence, he was another Thomas Smith – the same name as one of Watts' travelling companions. Engineer Smith allowed Watts to use the tools in his cabin to undertake some fretwork. This creative pastime involved cutting intricate patterns into wooden panels that were later used to decorate the home. Watts returned to his fretwork several times throughout the journey.

The *Victoria*'s eight-piece band was led by Fred Stabbins, with each of its members doubling as stewards. Its evening performances after dinner were rather like a modern 'disco', providing the opportunity for saloon passengers to dance, drink and socialise. Watts and his companions usually attended. The ship's officers – especially the more junior ones – might also join in. Watts' friend Mary, for example, was quite often in the company of the ship's third officer, Robert Hopkins, although the potential significance of this seems to have totally escaped Watts.

Passenger comforts were the joint responsibility of two senior officers, Mr Cleworth the purser and Mr Wallis the head steward, and P&O prided itself in providing a professional, yet friendly, service. However, the company was aware that some officers could become 'over familiar' with female passengers and warned captains to guard against this. This does not, however, seem to have hindered third officer Hopkins.

On 26 October the *Victoria* arrived at Malta. This was a traditional stop for ships to refuel – a noisy, time-consuming and rather messy business in which the vessel was attended by a procession of barges stacked with coal, so passengers were encouraged to go ashore and get out of the way. The crew assisted Watts and his four friends to make a party of eight with three other passengers, and they took a small boat to the island's capital, Valletta. They toured the sights – St John's Cathedral, the Grandmaster's Palace, the markets and the San Anton Gardens – and had an evening meal at the Imperial Hotel. Watts stayed ashore and took a box at the theatre where he found 'a great many others from the P&O'. For once Watts stayed up late – he didn't get back to the ship until midnight.

The ship sailed on in good weather and the passengers enjoyed views of the coast, including a glimpse of Mount Etna in Sicily. During this part of the voyage, the first engineer, Henry Hammett, took Watts and 11 other passengers down into the bowels of the ship to see her engines. Down here it was very hot and very noisy so that the engineer had to shout to be heard. The *Victoria* had been built by Caird & Company of Greenock in 1887. Her 7,000 horsepower triple-expansion steam engines were built by the same company; they drove a single propeller, and enabled the vessel to make a top speed of around 16 knots.

By today's standards, the *Victoria* provided a limited range of passenger services, and so personal interaction with the crew was a welcome diversion. Otherwise, passengers were largely left to entertain themselves. About once a week, Watts availed himself of the ship's barber, Thomas Gouldsmith – who attended to both sexes – and had his hair shampooed. Before the advent of shops on board, the barber often sold a few items to oblige passengers, as another passenger, Tom Smith, recorded on board the SS *Orizaba* in 1887:

'The barber's shop was quite an institution on board. In fact, the term "general emporium" would more correctly describe it. Anything could be obtained, from pipes to hairpins, from clothing of all sorts to chocolates and lollies.'

The ship also offered passengers the opportunity to host their own afternoon tea party; Watts hosted one during the voyage and was also invited to those organised by other passengers.

On 28 October, *Victoria* called at Brindisi in the 'heel' of Italy which acted as a hub for P&O ships to collect mail for Australia, China and India. It was also a refuelling stop. Watts again ventured ashore but this time found the ancient town rather uninspiring. On 31 October the vessel arrived at Port Said near the entrance to the Suez Canal, but his Brindisi experience having perhaps put him off a little, Watts decided not to leave the ship. However, he was fascinated to see *Victoria* enter the canal which had opened only 19 years before, and he stayed up until past midnight to watch them 'start down the canal by electric light' with the ship's searchlights blazing out to illuminate their way in the darkness. Before the use of electricity on ships, only a few years before, navigation of the narrow canal at night had simply been impossible.

The next morning, Watts was on deck as soon as possible to continue watching the ship's fascinating progress down the Suez Canal:

'Got up at 7.30 so as to see as much of the canal by daylight as I could. Very nice breeze in the morning. Went very slowly down all day. Got very warm about 11. Very much amused to see the Egyptian boys running along the side of the canal for miles for coppers and anything else they could get. Saw plenty of camels hard at work. Arrived at Suez at 7.30 in the evening. Nobody landed as we only stayed for about an hour.'

Even in the 1880s some steamships avoided the Suez Canal and continued to run the old sailing ship route to Australia via the southern tip of Africa, as taken by Mary Perston aboard the *Coleroon* in 1868. By stopping in Cape Town, such ships could take passengers and cargo to two continents, so increasing profitability, and William Lilley, whose account of a stowaway has already been mentioned, pursued this route on the SS *Orient* in 1883.

## The Red Sea Run to Adelaide

Once the ship reached the Red Sea, the temperatures started to soar and it soon became uncomfortably hot. Awnings were put up to offer the passengers some shade, but the crew had to continue working despite the heat: the decks were scrubbed every morning, the communal areas cleaned, bed linen changed in cabins, meals prepared and the engines stoked with coal. In the midst of this oppressive heat, a group of the ship's stewards put on a Christy Minstrels show on the second saloon deck. This type of performance involved white men 'blacking up' – as it was called – to look like Victorian society's stereotypical image of black men, with eyes and lips exaggerated with white or red face paint. They usually sang songs from the American south and sometimes clowned around or told jokes. All very offensive to modern tastes, but in the Victorian theatre this kind of entertainment was popular and common. Watts enjoyed it.

However, despite the entertainments on offer, the escalating temperatures started to become difficult for the passengers to tolerate, even though the *Victoria* was steaming ahead at full speed:

'Saturday 3rd: Still in the Red Sea. Getting hotter and hotter; obliged to have the punkas put up. Most of the people had to sleep on deck as their cabins were unbearable, but I thought it would perhaps be wisest for me to retire to my berth, consequently could not sleep at all. The heat was intense.'

The punka – another Anglo-Indian word, like tiffin – was a primitive form of air conditioning. Punkas consisted of large stretched sheets of canvas on wooden frames that were suspended above the passengers' heads in communal areas, then gently swung to and fro to circulate the air. Passengers were not allowed to 'dress down' in public because of the heat, which made the heat more difficult to bear, and the next day was not much better: 'Sunday 4th. Still intensely hot. The people do nothing else all the day but loll about in their deck–chairs keeping perfectly quiet, mopping their faces with eau de Cologne'.

At the port of Aden, on 5 November, the *Victoria* refuelled again but had to wait a few hours to meet her sister ship *Arcadia* which was heading to India. This allowed both ships to exchange mail and passengers for their respective destinations. During this stop, local tradesmen came on board to parade their wares:

'Very much amused all the day at the number of different men that came on board with things to sell: ostrich feathers and all kinds of Indian work. Watched the little blackies dive off the top of the boat for sixpence, and quantities of large fish jumping out of the water at a tremendous height.'

The temperature cooled a little after leaving the stifling waters of the Red Sea, and the *Victoria* headed into the Indian Ocean. During this leg of the voyage, the crew organised a fancy dress ball for the passengers. This was a fairly traditional on–board entertainment. Passengers were given notice to use their ingenuity to create a suitable costume from whatever they had with them or could find on the ship; the resources on board were somewhat limited but the vessel's barber could be of great assistance. Of course, not everyone chose to dress up:

'Dancing commenced after dinner at 8.30 and kept up until 12 o'clock. A very pretty sight: between 50 and 60 came dressed. A great many more meant to have turned up, but they had to retire to their cabins instead, the motion of the boat all the morning being too much for them. Mary went as an Italian gypsy and looked remarkably well. I went in ordinary evening dress like a great many of the others.'

On 11 November, the *Victoria* docked at Colombo, the capital of Sri Lanka (then called Ceylon) where the ship re-fuelled once more and parted with the mail for China that it had carried since Brindisi. Watts and his party decided to de-camp to the Oriental Hotel for an overnight stay and enjoyed exploring Colombo and its environs by carriage. The following day they were back on board *Victoria*.

It was traditional for passengers on long P&O cruises to organise an 'amusements committee' to help fill their days as enjoyably as possible. This was important during the long run from Colombo to Australia as there were no stops on the way. Watts attended the first committee meeting where they planned their entertainments – the first being a cricket match on the afternoon of 13 November. As improbable though it may sound, cricket was played on a coconut matting pitch, with nets strung out to prevent the ball falling into the sea. The next day, the committee organised a small concert under the direction of the Bishop of Nelson, at which Mary sang a song or two and played the piano, and this was followed by a ladies' cricket match, and another concert. This second concert was held on the hurricane deck because strong monsoon winds were making the seas rough.

Whether inspired by the stormy waves or not, Watts for once attended Sunday worship. He constantly makes excuses in his diary for avoiding religious observance and it was clearly an obligation that held very limited appeal for him. However, on this occasion he listened to a 'splendid sermon' from the Bishop. Every Sunday before the service, the crew were required to line up on deck in their best uniforms for inspection by the captain.

Throughout the voyage, Watts occasionally did some drawing and painting to amuse himself. He now embarked on a project to paint the SS *Victoria* herself. He borrowed a photograph from the ship's medical officer, Dr Powell, and spent several days perfecting his depiction, despite the increased motion of the vessel:

'Monday 19th: Finished painting "Victoria" in the morning. In the evening at 7.30 dinner, the ship all of a sudden began to roll very much and of course, not expecting it, it caused very great excitement all around the saloon, seeing the bottles upsetting in all directions, the plates, glasses etc sliding off the table in a most ridiculous manner. Continued to roll all night, consequently could not get hardly any sleep.'

The following day they made Australia: the *Victoria* nosed into King George Sound, the large bay in south west Australia that is part of the port of Albany. Once there, the ship was delayed waiting for the mail train to be repaired and Watts reports that on hearing this, *Victoria*'s captain, George Cates, was 'very much put out and annoyed'.

There was the opportunity to explore Albany but Watts was late again and missed the boat going ashore. However, the voyage was nearly at an end and he began to pack up his possessions. As a parting gift to the attentive Robert Hopkins, the third officer who had taken a shine to Mary, Watts painted the man's name on his trunk for him. On 25 November the *Victoria* docked at Adelaide – the end of their journey. Mary's uncle came to pick them up and was anxious to depart quickly but Watts was, of course, late getting ready, so eventually the others capitulated and they sat down to a final breakfast together on board before disembarking.

Later in Watts' diaries, when the *Victoria* returned to Adelaide in December, Mary insisted on breaking from their exploration of Australia to visit the ship and wish the crew well. Watts had at last cottoned on to the reasons for this, but he was still in for a shock as they left the vessel's side: 'On returning in the steam tug, Mary turns round quietly and says to me, "Do you know Mr Hopkins and I are engaged?" and my reply was, "No, not really," in utter astonishment'.

The phrase 'in utter astonishment' is underlined. Mary Witherby and Robert Hopkins married in India in 1891.

## Chapter Thirteen

# A Steerage Passenger to New York

## *(1896, Hubert Whitmarsh, SS* Lucania*)*

In a classic early example of undercover reporting, the journalist Hubert Phelps Whitmarsh played the part of a British steerage passenger to find out what conditions were like on board ships for Europeans emigrating to America. He later wrote up his experiences for an American publication, *Century Magazine*.

The identity of the ship that he travelled on has always been a mystery because Whitmarsh was careful not to reveal it in his article. His story was published in 1898, but research for this book, using passenger lists held by the National Archives at Kew, shows that the only H.P. Whitmarsh to cross the Atlantic from Liverpool to New York during this period was on board Cunard's SS *Lucania* in June 1896. He had to travel under his own name of course – to forge a new one would have broken the law – but the passenger records show that Whitmarsh simply invented a working class career as an unmarried 33-year-old labourer to satisfy the various officials he would encounter. He also had to adopt an appearance commensurate with his new identity: 'When I entered upon my role as emigrant, I provided myself with a well-worn suit of clothes, an old hat, and a flannel shirt. I allowed my beard to grow, eschewed collars and cuffs, and made myself up for the part'.

Two weeks before his departure he had written to the shipping company, Cunard, in Liverpool to secure a steerage passage to New York. He was obliged to pay a deposit of one pound, and to complete a questionnaire which requested basic information about himself, his finances and his line of work. Having answered to the steamship company's satisfaction, he received his ticket and boarded a train for Liverpool from his residence in Oxford.

At Liverpool, Whitmarsh made his way to the steerage offices in the dimly-lit basement of a large stone building near the docks. Here the company's agent took his final payment, stamped his ticket and issued his berth number. After this, he and many other emigrants were led to a landing stage where they boarded a tender to take them up the river Mersey to their liner *Lucania*. Once there, they waited, marvelling at the sheer size of the liner towering next to them, before the moment came to board. Yet despite Whitmarsh's careful disguise he wasn't immediately recognised as a steerage passenger and was assumed to be travelling second class:

> 'A small army of stewards lined up to receive us, the gang-plank was lowered, and we filed aboard. "Second cabin, sir?" said the master-at-arms by the gangway. "No, steerage," I replied. His polite tone changed, and he invited me to "step for'ard lively!" in a manner that left no doubt in my mind as to what part of the ship I belonged'.

## Steerage Quarters

It was Saturday, 20 June 1896, and over 300 steerage passengers had boarded *Lucania* at the same time as Whitmarsh. Predictably, the narrow corridor ahead of them was soon blocked by all the people crowded into it with their carry-on luggage. The crew became irritated and the passengers were 'driven, pushed and sworn at' – treated like cattle, in fact – but eventually they made it down a steep flight of stairs where Whitmarsh was allocated his bunk. There were different compartments for different types of steerage passenger – single English-speaking men, single foreign men, married couples, and single women. Whitmarsh describes his accommodation which he occupied with 117 other men:

> 'Steerage No. 1 is virtually in the eyes of the vessel, and runs clear across from one side to the other, without a partition. It is lighted entirely by portholes, under which, fixed to the stringers, are narrow tables with benches before them. The remaining space is filled with iron bunks, row after row, tier upon tier, all running fore and aft in double banks. A thin iron rod is all that separates one sleeper from another. In each bunk are placed 'a donkey's breakfast' (a straw mattress), a blanket of the horse variety, a battered tin plate and pannikin, a knife, a fork, and a spoon. This completes the emigrant's 'kit', which in former days had to be found by himself.'

However, perhaps to his surprise, Whitmarsh noted that their gloomy accommodation was not dirty: 'To the credit of the ship, it must be said that everything was clean. Sweet it was not. Spotless, sanded decks, scrubbed paintwork, and iron bunks could not hide the sour, shippy, reminiscent odour that hung about the steerages, one and all'.

Each passenger had limited space, and soon every bed was piled with clothing, bags, food and bottles. But before they could get too comfortable, they were mustered for inspection by the ship's doctor:

'Evidently the doctor was in no hurry: for we stood crowded together in the heat of that summer day two mortal hours waiting his pleasure. Poor mothers! Poor babies! Tired, hot, and hungry (for no dinner had been served) the little ones cried incessantly, while the women complained in a high key, and twelve nationalities of men swore.'

The claustrophobia of their quarters was magnified by the fact that they were confined with very limited access to daylight, apart from a square of deck around the after-hatch. The space in which they could actually walk was quite restricted and once the ship set sail 'half of it was roped off to keep us from going too near the saloon passengers' windows'.

All of this contrasts rather vividly with the facilities provided for first class passengers on the *Lucania*, as described by Henry Fry:

'The accommodations for passengers are sumptuous... The dining saloon is a vast, lofty apartment, near the middle of the ship, 100 feet long, 62 feet broad, and 10 feet high, capable of seating at dinner 430 passengers in revolving armchairs. The decorations are highly artistic: the ceiling is panelled in white and gold; the sides in Spanish mahogany; and the upholstering is in a dark, rich red figured frieze velvet, with curtains to match... The drawing-room is a splendid apartment, 60 x 30 feet. The walls are in satinwood, relieved with cedar mouldings; the ceiling is in pine, decorated in light tones, in which old ivory and gilding prevail. The settees, ottomans and chairs are upholstered in rich velvets and brocades which, with a Persian carpet, brass firegrate, and hearth of Persian tiles, form a superb 'tout ensemble'. A grand piano and an American organ are also provided.

'The staterooms are lofty and well ventilated. The old wooden coffin-like berth has been superseded by Hopkins' 'triptic' beds, which are so constructed that the upper bed folds up against the bulkhead... There are rooms suited to all tastes; single and double berth cabins and family rooms. For those who do not mind the cost, there are suites of rooms fitted in satinwood and mahogany, with everything to match; parlour and bedroom, the former fitted up with tables and chairs after the style of a lady's boudoir; the latter fitted with a brass bedstead, hangings, wardrobe, etc. There are also staterooms fitted with a collapsible bedstead, or with one capable of being extended so as to form a double bed, and which, when used as a single one, may be converted into a couch and settee.'

## The Journey Begins

Two tugs escorted the *Lucania* downstream to a landing stage where the saloon passengers were taken on board. A warning bell was sounded to indicate that visitors should go ashore, and soon the liner was being edged from the pier by her tugs. Whitmarsh witnessed the agony as some steerage passengers realised they were leaving their friends, families and homes forever, but within minutes they heard the ship's screws turning and *Lucania* began to speed down the river. By 8 pm they were already in the Irish Sea and the Welsh coastline sped by in the gathering darkness.

When Whitmarsh retired for the night he was pleased to find that he had a top bunk, but his berth was the middle one of a row of five, with just the thin metal rod between neighbours. He was disconcerted by this lack of privacy and eyed his unknown sleeping companions with suspicion:

'A few of the men had taken their coats off and placed them under their heads for pillows; but most lay as they had stood, with boots, coats, and, in many cases, their caps on. After building a barricade of bags and blankets on each side, I lay down in the middle, and got a few hours' sleep. One night of it, however, was sufficient. For the remainder of the passage, I slept on deck.'

At four o'clock the next morning they were awakened by the ship docking at Queenstown in Ireland (now known as Cobh). Around 70 extra steerage passengers joined them – mainly young Irish girls – and once boarded, they began to dance and sing to the accompaniment of an accordion. Before long various other passengers with instruments joined in and soon the compartment was filled with music, dancing and song. These spontaneous entertainments were to break out frequently during their time together.

As was the case for other classes of passenger, food was provided to steerage at set times and this helped to structure people's day. Each meal on board was announced by the ringing of a hand-bell and a 'bawling steward':

'At eight o'clock each morning we were served with oatmeal, coffee, soft bread, and butter. Every other morning Irish stew was added. For dinner we received excellent soup, one kind of meat or fish, with potatoes and bread. Twice we had steamed pudding. For supper we contented ourselves with bread and butter and tea. I must say that the tea was remindful of chopped corn-brooms, and that the coffee was an unadulterated abomination; but the remainder of the food was plain, wholesome fare, clean and of good quality.'

Despite the standard of the food, Whitmarsh regretted that it was simply 'slung at you' from a large slop bucket or similar container, since the manner of its serving and presentation made it seem less appetising.

Most of Sunday was spent in smooth water, running under the lee of the Irish coast. The warm weather encouraged people to occupy their small deck space by the after-hatch, but with over 400 steerage passengers, the area quickly became crowded. Unlike first and second class, where so much entertainment was organised and amenities provided, nothing was offered to help steerage passengers while away their time and there was little they could do to occupy themselves: 'Men, women, and children all crowded about the after- hatch, some playing cards, some dancing, and some already making love; but for the most part they lay about the deck, sleeping and basking in the sun'.

Late Sunday evening, the *Lucania* rounded Fastnet and entered the Atlantic. The sea was not stormy but a keen northwest wind kept the waves large, and the deep ocean swell took its toll on the steerage. Seasickness is a miserable experience at the best of times but in a dark, crowded space deep in the bowels of the ship, it seemed to take on an extra intensity. There was no early sign of relief either, and in the end it lasted for two days. Whitmarsh and a small number of men who weren't affected passed the time 'spinning yarns and burning unlimited tobacco'.

However, by Tuesday the weather had settled and the rest of their passage was a lot easier on passengers' stomachs. Tuesday also saw the 'much-dreaded' vaccination muster. It was the law at this time that no-one could enter America without having been vaccinated against smallpox. This meant that the steerage passengers had once more to line up before the ship's doctor. All who could show him a vaccination scar on their arm satisfied him. Those who could not, or whose scar was indistinct, were vaccinated. One passenger refused, but he relented on being told he could not enter America without it.

## Passenger Origins and Behaviour

Helpfully, Whitmarsh provides a breakdown of the 403 steerage passengers by nationality. There were 189 people from Great Britain:

| | |
|---|---|
| English | 51 |
| Irish | 113 |
| Scottish | 4 |
| Welsh | 21 |

And the remaining passengers came from various countries, but with Scandinavia predominating:

| | |
|---|---|
| American | 59 |
| Bohemian | 1 |
| Finnish | 43 |
| French | 1 |
| German | 7 |
| Norwegian | 25 |
| Russian | 1 |
| Swedish | 77 |

Whitmarsh estimated that around two-thirds of the steerage passengers were men, and the majority were over 30 years old. 'Most of them were men of a restless disposition,' he notes, 'or were failures going to start afresh and try their luck in the new country'. His observations of the passengers on board ship suggested to him that many of the passengers would not be considered very desirable immigrants into America:

'The type of emigrant as a whole was, to me, sadly disappointing; and I am forced to admit that the worst class on board our vessel at least were those who hailed from Great Britain. For while among the Scandinavians there was a goodly percentage of sturdy, honest farm labourers and mechanics, it was very evident that those from the British Isles were adventurers, floaters, scum – a brotherhood, indeed, that needs no augmentation in this or any other country.'

However, it should be noted that Whitmarsh was writing for a mainly American audience, and it is not entirely clear what particular aspects of British passengers' behaviour or appearance led him to mark them out so unfavourably. In fact, over the course of his journey, Whitmarsh meets a number of British characters whom he describes with some affection, or at least without criticism: an Irishman taking a shamrock plant to give to his son in California, for example; a boilermaker from Birmingham who was the 'sunlight of the steerage' with his cheerful tin whistle. There was a dark, thickset Welshman with his thin wife and their five very dirty children; a Salvation Army sergeant; a red-faced man from Nottingham and his family who were going to open a bar in Pittsburgh; and a dour-looking, long-legged Scottish farmer who kept arguing about religion and politics.

Nonetheless, Whitmarsh was amazed at how many of the steerage passengers began to allow 'their baser natures to run riot' and perhaps it was in this respect that he noted a British dominance. The steerage quickly formed its own community with ways of behaving in public that appalled him:

'No sooner has the seasickness left them than they growl and snarl over their food like dogs, scrambling for the choice pieces, and running off to their bunks with them; they grow quarrelsome; their talk is lewd and insulting; brute strength is in the ascendant; and, without shame, both sexes show the animal side of their natures. But most apparent and obnoxious are the filthy habits into which many of them fall. The sea seems utterly to demoralize them. Some of them will remain for days in their berths, where, without changing their clothes, they eat, sleep, and are sick with the utmost impartiality, and without the blessing of soap and water. Hence the steerage as a whole, the married quarters (where there were children) in particular, was ill-smelling and otherwise objectionable.'

At nine o'clock every evening the night watchman made his rounds and sent all the female passengers to their separate sleeping quarters. He had a very difficult job because passengers who had quickly formed relationships with members of the opposite sex were loathe to be parted. Sometimes it took him over an hour to chase and catch all the women and escort them away.

The steerage passengers were not allowed to interact with the other classes of passenger on board – or, more correctly, they were segregated from them. Occasionally, first class passengers on the upper decks would look down on the crowded steerage deck space and throw food or money in appreciation of their lowly fellow travellers' singing or other performances. Needless to say, the crowd scrabbling for these favours turned steerage into what Whitmarsh calls a 'bear pit'. Yet perhaps this pitiable snatching after rich people's spare food or loose change was part of the attraction for those who bestowed them.

Whitmarsh also relates the tale of a well-bred woman who insisted on visiting steerage, and when amongst them all, asked her companions in a loud voice: "What makes them smell so?". Whitmarsh was as incensed as his fellow travellers.

All of this helped to fuel a desire amongst some of the men to visit the saloon decks. Whitmarsh and five others dodged the watchman at 10 o'clock one night and sneaked up the ladder that would take them to the second saloon. For a few moments they enjoyed the pristine white decks, polished brass, music and fresh air of what seemed like paradise. They even peeked in at the saloon passengers enjoying an evening concert. But they were soon accosted by a member of the crew and 'driven ignominiously back to our own pen'.

## New York in Sight

Thursday morning brought rare excitement for the whole ship, including steerage: on the far horizon ahead of them, the telltale signs of a steamship from a rival company. The prospect of a race set steerage buzzing with speculation. The other ship is not identified but given the great competition at this time between Cunard, who owned the *Lucania*, and the White Star company, it may have been one of the latter's vessels. The *Lucania* made all speed and gradually caught and then passed the other ship.

Crews were very proud of their ship, and captains went to great efforts to emerge victorious in these races, which were quite common. It made good publicity for the company when they won, and the competitive attitude helped to stimulate the technological innovation that produced ever-faster ships. No doubt there were wagers made, and cheering as the Cunarder overhauled her opponent.

Passing its rival brought the ship into fog off the east coast of America, and soon all thoughts were turned to reaching their final destination, New York. It was now Friday morning, but would they get ashore by Friday night or would it be Saturday morning? An eager, buzzing crowd watched the land draw nearer and wondered what the future would hold for them.

An hour after sunset, the *Lucania* docked at her pier. The steerage passengers were prevented from disembarking, while those in first and second class made their way ashore. Steamship companies were responsible for the immigrants that they brought into America, and could be fined if any escaped ashore before being assessed by the proper authorities. Unfortunately, the steerage passengers were detained on board until morning – enduring a final hot and uncomfortable night – and were further delayed when a steamer blocked their exit route.

Eventually at eleven o'clock on Saturday morning, Whitmarsh and his fellow passengers were allowed onto the pier. There were further delays while their luggage was inspected by customs officials, leaving the people to stand and fume in the baking summer heat. After two hours of this, a barge came to take them down river to the immigration offices at Ellis Island. It took until five o'clock in the evening to clear all the formalities – they were inspected by a doctor once more, had to reveal what money they had brought with them, and were then interviewed about their past, present and future lives. Paupers, lunatics and those incapable of earning a living were sent straight back home at the expense of the steamship company that brought them. Whitmarsh reports that between 1 July 1895 and 30 June 1896, a total of 343,267 immigrants were assessed at Ellis Island, of whom 2,799 were returned.

Whitmarsh summarises his experiences in steerage with this observation:

'The ship's company shoved me along the decks and swore at me without prejudice; the saloon and second-cabin passengers who occasionally stepped gingerly and curiously into our quarters looked me squarely in the eyes without a sign of recognition; and the steerage simply opened its dirty arms and took me in without a question.'

But the experience did make him reflect. 'Personally,' he says, 'I consider a trip in the steerage an excellent thing for a man. It knocks the conceit out of him'.

*Chapter Fourteen*

# An Infamous Casualty of War

## *(1915, Phoebe Amory, RMS* Lusitania*)*

Phoebe Amory lived in Canada but she had five sons who had enlisted in the British Army to fight in the Great War and, at 65 years of age, decided to travel to the UK to be near them. She wondered if this reunion might be their last as she was advancing in years and it was not clear how long the war would continue.

On 27 April 1915, she visited an agent's office in Toronto and bought a second class ticket to England. The next available ship was Cunard's *Lusitania* and Mrs Amory must have been delighted at the prospect of travelling on this prestigious liner. Launched in 1906, *Lusitania* was the first British ship to sport four funnels and was one of the largest vessels in the world at 31,550 tons. Its world-renowned sumptuous interiors and on board elegance merited the title, 'floating palace', and it had the best accommodation afloat for its 2,198 passengers. It was a reliable ship, too, having completed over 200 Atlantic crossings by the time Mrs Amory booked her passage. *Lusitania*'s engines had an output of 76,000 horsepower, driving four huge propellers, to reach top speeds in excess of 26 knots. To put this in perspective: 50 years earlier in 1858, Reverend Neville's *Armenian* (Chapter 9) had one small propeller, a 200 horsepower engine, and a top speed of nine knots.

The *Lusitania* was due to depart on 1 May. This gave Mrs Amory just enough time to pack and reach New York for the sailing. Perhaps it was the rush to be there on time, but Mrs Amory raced on board without buying a newspaper. Had she done so, she would have discovered a warning from the German Embassy in all the dailies. This advert reminded passengers that Germany and Britain were at war; that the *Lusitania* was a British ship, and so would be considered a legitimate U-boat target in European waters. Travellers were advised that if they embarked on *Lusitania*, they did so at their own risk. Some passengers were even warned in person by Germans on the quayside.

Mrs Amory only learned of these warnings once she was safely aboard, but was undeterred. Some passengers did, in fact, cancel their booking, and the *Lusitania* departed with 1,264 passengers: more than 900 less than she could carry. However, many people believed the Germans would not dare to attack a liner; especially one carrying passengers from America, a neutral country in the war. Others were confident that *Lusitania* was fast enough to outrun any U-boat. This was, after all, the first ship in the world to cross the Atlantic in under five days.

What the passengers didn't know was that the war had mandated a reduced crew and a need to economise on coal, so one of *Lusitania*'s four boiler rooms had been shut down. This meant that the ship's speed was reduced to a maximum of around 21 knots, with a 'cruising' speed of around 18 knots.

## Making Ready to Sail

Mrs Amory walked to her cabin with a porter who took her luggage for her. Because she was travelling second class, she would share her cabin with two other women, who had not yet arrived. Second class cabins on *Lusitania* accommodated two, three or four passengers, and there were so many rooms that they occupied a full 150 feet of the length of the ship. Each cabin had bunk beds with mattresses, and plain wooden panelling on the walls to hide the structure of the ship. The walls and ceilings were painted white, and there was a patterned carpet, a washstand and mirror, and an electric light.

Mrs Amory had always enjoyed the sights of a busy port and watching a ship preparing to sail, so she found a convenient vantage point and surveyed all the goings-on. The dock was crowded with relatives, friends and well-wishers waiting to see the liner off, and gazing up at the sheer black hull, the white decks and the four black-topped bright red funnels. Passengers crossed the gangways or bridges onto the *Lusitania*'s decks; officers gave their orders; trucks of luggage and mail were rushed on board; port officials brought their paperwork. Then suddenly the bells alerting non-passengers to leave were sounded, and they were ready to depart:

'The shrill blasts from tug-boats announced that they were ready to begin their labor of moving the great ship from her moorings, and the deep, throaty reply from the chimes of the Lusitania voiced her assent. Bridges were swung. Two more sharp exchanges of signals from the tugs, and we were moving. The mightiest vessel in the world had started on what was to be her last voyage.'

The ship's band struck up as the vessel moved off, and a choir on board started to sing. The passengers and well-wishers cheered, and waved hats, flags and handkerchiefs at one another. The *Lusitania*'s departure had been delayed because she was obliged to take 41 passengers from another liner – the *Cameronia* – which had been requisitioned for the war effort by the Royal Navy. But now the wait was over, and they passed down the Hudson River, where the tugs left them, and headed out into the ocean where *Lusitania* rapidly gathered speed.

The ship was commanded by gruff, yet experienced, William Turner who was Cunard's commodore – its most senior officer. He was not a charismatic man, and unlike many captains who made the most of their on-board 'celebrity' status, Turner did not relish socialising with passengers; he tended to avoid them when he could.

## Life on Board

Having watched the land slip away astern, Mrs Amory returned to her cabin; all the fresh air and excitement had given her an appetite and she was also keen to meet her cabin-mates. Fortunately, both of her new companions were 'very charming ladies'. There was a younger, attractive girl called Mary Higginbottom, and a widow of similar age to Mrs Amory, Martha Whyatt. Once the three ladies had their room arranged to their mutual liking, Mary asked Mrs Amory to dinner and they made their way to the eating area:

'Such a beautiful dining room I had never seen, either aboard ship, or in the magnificent hotels that I have seen on both sides of the ocean. The pillars, extending from floor to ceiling, were as snowy white as the linen that covered the long tables. The walls and ceilings were frescoed in delicate tints, and in the centre there was a round, open balcony, which permitted one to stand above and gaze down upon a spectacle that I believe could not be duplicated elsewhere.'

Although *Lusitania* was light on passengers generally, there were a disproportionately large number of people travelling second class – six hundred, in fact: almost half the total. So whilst other passenger sections were relatively quiet, second class was busy. They therefore had to wait for the second seating for dinner, and some passengers even had to sit in the passageway, but not Mrs Amory. They sat at long tables in beautifully upholstered swivel chairs and admired the profusion of palm trees in the oak-panelled dining area, including one that nearly reached to the very high ceiling.

A second-class menu from a previous voyage illustrates some of the typical fare on offer:

---

*MENU*

———

*Main courses:*
*Salmon trout, Dutch sauce*
*Steak and kidney pudding*
*Braised veal, lemon sauce*
*Roast turkey, bread sauce*
*Corned ox tongue, carrots*
*Cold, boiled ham*
*Side dishes: boiled rice, purée of turnips, boiled potatoes*

*Desserts:*
*Damson tart*
*Gelée custard*
*Macaroon torten*
*Saxon pudding*
*Ice cream*

*To follow:*
*Cheese*
*Tea or coffee*

---

The second class facilities on *Lusitania* were second to none. In fact, second class on *Lusitania* was at least equal to first class on some other shipping lines. Passengers had their own lounges, library and smoking room. In accordance with the palatial style for liners of the period, *Lusitania*'s public rooms were decorated and furnished lavishly in a broadly Renaissance style. There were also promenade decks at the stern end of the upper decks reserved for second class passengers, and although not as large as those allocated to first class, they did offer an air of exclusivity. But this was not yet the era of casinos, cinemas and on board shopping malls.

The segregation of passengers at sea by class was still very strict. The first, second and third classes of accommodation mirrored the basic structure of early twentieth century society – upper, middle and lower – and these groups of passengers were expected to stay separate or the crew would intervene, as Hubert Whitmarsh had recounted as a steerage passenger 20 years before. A children's book from 1922 explains it all:

'A tour of inspection of the ship is always interesting, but it is very bad form to gratify idle curiosity by examining the quarters of other classes of passengers, as such intrusion is naturally resented. Each class has its own quarters and it is a breach of the unwritten rules of etiquette at sea for passengers of one class to enter another class unless specially invited, such as to a concert or other entertainment.'

The three classes had very different facilities and staffing. Crossing the boundary could breed resentment if one class came face-to-face with the superior privileges of another. Mingling between classes was seen as simply inviting trouble, as Miss Perston noted in 1868 (Chapter 11), and sharp words or conflict in the close confines of an ocean-going vessel were things to be avoided.

As night fell, stewards came to check that passengers had drawn curtains over their portholes. The *Lusitania* ran with minimum lighting at night to hinder detection by U-boats. As a precaution, Captain Turner also set extra lookouts, and kept some of the lifeboats swung out to aid speedy launching. Unlike the *Titanic* three years before, the *Lusitania* had sufficient places in its lifeboats to carry everyone on board.

During the first few days of the voyage, Mrs Amory came to admire her roommate, Mrs Whyatt, who was kindly and always ready to help others. She seemed to have at her disposal everything needed for those suffering from seasickness, and appeared to spend most of her time tending to fellow passengers.

Otherwise, the passengers occupied themselves with all the usual on-board pursuits – dining, reading, writing, relaxing, deck games and so on. However, Mrs Amory particularly drew attention to a concert given for first and second class passengers on Thursday, 6 May in aid of the Seamen's Fund. Mid-Atlantic concerts of this nature had become something of a tradition by the twentieth century. With assistance from some of the crew and the ship's choir, a group of passengers put together a concert programme that included singing, piano recitals, jokes and other performances. Mrs Amory offered to sell the programmes that had been printed on board. She started with the first class cabins and staterooms, and despite her first customer having already purchased a programme elsewhere, he generously bought a second for five dollars and refused to take any change. She later learned that he was the American multi-millionaire Alfred Vanderbilt.

The concert went very well, Mrs Amory especially noting the performance of a young passenger named Mary who sang a song called *The Rosary*, and they raised nearly £20 for the seamen's charity. During the interval, Captain Turner gave a speech to thank the passengers for travelling on *Lusitania*. He assured them they would arrive safely in Liverpool on Saturday morning.

## The Fateful Day

Friday was the seventh day since leaving New York and Mrs Amory rose early to enjoy the early morning on deck. They were nearing Ireland, and whilst the early morning had been foggy, the sun was now bright and the sea beautifully smooth. 'We were very happy,' she wrote, 'in thinking that the remainder of our voyage would be made under favourable weather conditions, and that before another sunrise we would be landed and our journey completed'.

Mrs Whyatt had been ill all night, so Mrs Amory persuaded her to get dressed and helped her on deck to enjoy the fine weather. This simple act of kindness undoubtedly saved her roommate's life because, being on deck when the ship went down, she was one of the first to be saved.

At noon, the bell sounded for first lunch but Mrs Amory had warmed herself in the sun and didn't feel hungry, so she decided to have a bath and go to second lunch. She had scarcely finished her bath when second lunch was called. Fortunately, the ship's dress code allowed passengers to attend lunch in informal attire, so she slipped a raincoat over her negligée, and hurried to the dining area. She now had an appetite:

> 'I took my place at table, and had given my order. It then occurred to me that I would like a salad, and as the steward placed the soup before me I was on the point of ordering the salad when there came the most terrible crash, which seemed to tear everything to pieces, and to rend the ship asunder.'

Some passengers on deck enjoying the weather later reported seeing the German submarine's conning tower a few hundred yards to starboard, and then the torpedo that U-boat number 20 fired, as it raced toward them. The torpedo struck *Lusitania* below the bridge, slightly forward of the ship's first funnel. It was just after 2 pm.

Meanwhile in the second class dining room, passengers raced for the exit. Mrs Amory pushed her way through the tightly packed, fearful crowd that blocked the stairway to the upper decks.

> 'Someone shouted, "We have been torpedoed", and I realized for the first time that we were doomed. As I fought my way up the stairs, I was thrown on my knees three times. Near the top of the stairway there was an officer shouting 'keep cool', and his words seemed to have the desired effect as the terrible crush subsided, and those of us who were nearing the top found it less difficult to ascend.'

The ship began to list heavily, and Mrs Amory feared that the liner would capsize. It seemed to take hours to reach the deck and fresh air, but in reality it was just a few minutes. Once there, the unnatural slope of the deck was disconcerting, and she worried about falling over the side. The list also hampered the launching of lifeboats because they either swung away from the deck, out of reach, or swung in-board so that it was difficult to lower them into the water.

'The screams of the women and children were terrible to hear. Wives were being torn from their husbands and lifted into the lifeboats. Children, who in the terrible crush of humans, had become separated from their parents, were being handed from man to man and on into the boats. Women were fainting and falling to the deck, only to be carried overboard by their own weight.'

As the slope of the decks increased, Mrs Amory searched for a lifebelt, reasoning it was her only chance of survival as she could not reach the boats. Just as she had given up hope, a young man grabbed her and bravely handed her his own lifebelt. He helped her into it and adjusted it for her. She thanked him, but when she turned to speak to him properly he had gone. Mrs Amory later hunted for him amongst the survivors but he was not there. One of many acts of self-sacrifice on that day.

The lifeboats were rapidly filling and being launched. As the last boat was being prepared, an officer spied Mrs Amory further back and ordered the male passengers to let her through. 'The last boat is leaving,' he said, 'and this lady must go'. He took her by the hand and led her to the rail, but the list of the ship was such that the lifeboat had swung too far out for her, so she had to jump. She landed on the boat but its descent was suddenly checked as it crashed into the hull of the *Lusitania* – either the great liner had rolled or the lifeboat's lowering ropes had snagged. The result was that the lifeboat passengers were thrown into the water. Those without lifebelts quickly drowned, 'On every hand were floating bodies, their upturned faces showing white and ghastly'.

Mrs Amory landed close to the *Lusitania*'s side but waves soon bore her away. She floated on her back – an uncomfortable sensation, but she could not turn over. Wearing only a raincoat, negligée, stockings and shoes, the cold Atlantic waves washed over her, filling her mouth with water, and she began to despair of being rescued:

'Each time a bit of wreckage would float against me I would take courage
and think that a boat was near and that they were trying to reach me,
but when the drift would float by I would again be possessed of the
fear that I was destined to float around until I could no longer survive,
and then die. I could see myself being washed ashore a lifeless corpse.'

Very few of *Lusitania*'s lifeboats had been launched with complete success.
Most couldn't be launched; some had tipped their passengers into the sea on
lowering because of the *Lusitania*'s list, and, distressingly, some were filled
with passengers and still secured to the liner as it went down.

Suddenly a sharp object touched Mrs Amory's neck and then her head
was jerked up by a man wielding a boathook. A lifeboat had spotted her grey
hair, and despite being fully loaded, had taken pity on the older woman and
determined to rescue her. 'I was overjoyed and could think of nothing to say
but "Thank God, thank God, I am being saved".'

However, the lifeboat occupants were worried about overturning their
boat, so Mrs Amory was pulled only halfway in, so that her legs dangled in
the water. She stayed in this position for some time until her legs went numb,
but despite the pain she was so grateful that she said nothing. Eventually
they managed to move people around in the lifeboat to redistribute the
passengers' weight, and Mrs Amory was heaved aboard.

'I raised my head just in time to see the last of the Lusitania as she
sank beneath the waves. As she sank, there was a mighty rush of water
and we were rocked until we nearly capsized, but the men who were
handling our boat were expert seamen, and after a moment of anxiety
as to our being able to survive the heavy wash, we righted again, and
the men took to the oars.'

Bodies floated past them – men, women and children – 'it was terrible to
look upon children, oh, such little children, floating away out there on the
ocean'. Mrs Amory felt anger towards the perpetrators but also gratitude at
her own survival, and the lifeboat occupants gave thanks by prayer.

Eleven miles off the coast of southern Ireland, they rowed for three or four
hours until they sighted a fishing boat. The passengers shouted themselves

hoarse trying to attract attention, and soon it was heading their way. Within a short time they were on the dirty, smelly craft, 'but,' as Mrs Amory remarks, 'never did a ship of any description look so good to me'. She collapsed in the boat as soon as they were on board but was revived by a cup of hot tea: 'The tea helped to warm me up considerably, but my teeth chattered and my limbs shook as though afflicted with the ague'.

They were soon intercepted by a cutter, which was a larger vessel, and all the survivors were transferred. Mrs Amory was so weak that she had to be carried aboard, but she had the pleasure of recognising many friends from the *Lusitania* who had been picked up earlier. A stewardess dried her clothes and Mrs Amory drank more tea, so that by time they sighted land she was in fairly good shape.

Once ashore, she watched with a combination of joy and pity as survivors searched for friends and family amongst the crowd who had been rescued. Mrs Amory broke down in tears as she witnessed the intense suffering of bereaved mothers, wives and husbands: 'Those bowed heads, the trembling bodies as sob after sob came forth, were more than I could bear, and I collapsed'.

Poignantly, her older roommate Mrs Whyatt survived, but not the young and pretty Mary Higginbottom. One young man approached Mrs Amory and revealed that it was his wife who had sung *The Rosary* during the *Lusitania*'s concert. She too had died. He swore to join the army and fight the Germans to seek revenge for his wife's murder.

Mrs Amory made it to Queenstown (modern Cobh) in Ireland, where she was given a clean suit of clothes and hastily made her way to England so that her sons could support her through the aftermath of this horrendous experience. And what did Mrs Amory think of the Germans on the U-boat that had torpedoed the *Lusitania*? 'That it was murder we cannot doubt, and for this murder we must have what reparation we can get by decisively defeating the perpetrators of such a dastardly and cowardly deed'.

There are many controversies surrounding the loss of the *Lusitania* but the significant human cost is very clear: the sinking was responsible for the deaths of around 1,200 passengers and crew. Yet, miraculously, despite the ship going down in just 18 minutes, 764 people were rescued and survived. The outrage from the American government, which had lost over 100 citizens aboard the liner, helped pave the way for the USA to enter the war.

*Chapter Fifteen*

# World Cruise in Luxury

## *(1926, Percy Shaw Jeffrey,* Empress of Scotland*)*

Percy Shaw Jeffrey was a retired headmaster who enjoyed travel. On Friday, 13 November 1926, aged 64, he and his wife Alice joined fellow passengers on board the *Empress of Scotland*. The couple had taken a special boat train from London Waterloo that carried them to virtually the ship's side while she was docked at Southampton. This was to be the fourth world cruise of the *Empress* at a time when commercial circumnavigation of the globe was still something of a novelty.

However, world cruises for personal pleasure were not new. Earlier in the nineteenth century it was possible to take such a voyage. Yet before the Panama Canal opened, most passengers – and shipping lines – were not prepared to risk lives in rounding the treacherous Cape Horn at the southern tip of South America. Nonetheless, some intrepid passengers did take this on, utilising privately owned vessels. In 1876, for example, Annie Brassey sailed round the world on the steam schooner *Sunbeam* which was owned by her husband. There were 11 passengers and a crew of around 30, and their circumnavigation took 11 months. They rounded South America successfully but had to rescue the crew of another vessel in distress near the Cape.

With the Cape Horn route discounted for most passengers, a commercial 'world cruise' on a steamship before the opening of the Panama Canal involved sailing until arrival at one of the North American ports. Passengers would then disembark, cross that continent by train, then board a new ship on the other side to continue the voyage. For example, William Lever published his account of such an experience: in 1892 he crossed the Atlantic to New York aboard the White Star liner *Germanic*; he then traversed the United States by rail before departing San Francisco on the SS *Australia* to continue his world cruise.

However, round the world trips could require complex scheduling. Lord Northcliffe's world cruise in 1921–22 required him to take no less than 13 steamships. He began by taking RMS *Aquitania* from Southampton to New York, then travelling by rail across Canada to the west coast. From here he took SS *Makura* to New Zealand, then SS *Maheno* to Australia, SS *St Albans* to Japan, SS *Nyanza* to Singapore, SS *Rumphius* to Indonesia, SS *Siberg* back to Singapore, SS *Amiral Latouche Tréville* to Vietnam, SS *Donai* to Thailand, SS *Nellore* to Sri Lanka, SS *Curzon* to India, SS *Naldera* to Egypt, and finally SS *Egypt* to France. And this itinerary did not include the several local vessels Lord Northcliffe's party used for short coastal trips to reach the next port from which his connecting ocean-going steamship operated.

The need to risk Cape Horn, cross North America by rail, or schedule complex multi-ship itineraries disappeared when the Panama Canal became available to passenger ships. The first commercial liner to exploit the Canal to take holidaying passengers completely around the world in a single trip was Cunard's *Laconia* in 1922–23, and an account of that voyage was published by an American passenger, Joel Burdick. This successful enterprise was quickly followed by other companies advertising a 'world cruise without change of ship'. Interestingly, the route pursued by the *Laconia* was very similar to that taken by Jeffrey aboard the *Empress of Scotland* only four years later.

Despite Cunard operating the first world holiday cruise by steamship, it must be said that during the 1920s the shipping line Canadian Pacific, owner of the *Empress of Scotland*, was at the forefront of world cruising. This company had a fleet of luxury ships and an eye on the richest end of the travel market: the cheapest fare for a world cruise on the *Empress of Scotland* was £460, at a time when the average wage for a man in the UK was about £5 per week. A deluxe apartment on the *Empress* cost more than £2,000 per head. In practice this meant that many world travellers were affluent Americans, but the experience was also popular amongst wealthy Britons and Canadians.

Their popularity in North America meant that world cruises often began officially from a US port, so British travellers might need to sail to America first before embarking. Alternatively, as was the case with Jeffrey's *Empress of Scotland*, the ship sailed from Southampton to Quebec and New York, but then re-crossed the Atlantic back to Europe to initiate its world cruise. Jeffrey's cruise itinerary was thus as follows:

Southampton – Cherbourg – Quebec – New York – Madeira – Gibraltar – Algiers – Italy – Palestine – Cairo – Suez Canal – India – Sri Lanka – Indonesia – Singapore – Philippines – China – Japan – Hawaii – San Francisco – Panama Canal – Cuba – New York – Quebec – Cherbourg – Southampton.

The early world cruises all tended to follow a similar route and to bypass Australasia. In 1931–32, for example, another Canadian Pacific passenger, Marion Bridie, published an account of her world trip and it followed the same course as Jeffrey. The timing of the *Empress*'s departure was scheduled to take advantage of a favourable local climate at each of the major destinations visited: North Africa and Palestine in the winter when it was less hot; India in its coolest month and outside the monsoon season; China and Japan in the spring, and returning to Southampton in time for the English summer. Jeffrey's cruise was also organised so that passengers might spend Christmas in Palestine, 'the Holy Land'.

### First Few Days

The *Empress* was powered by oil, consuming 240 tons of it every day at a cost in 1926 of over £5,000 per week. Oil was first utilised as an alternative ship's fuel to coal in the 1880s and was less dirty and more efficient, obviating the need for frequent messy and time-consuming stops for coaling. Oil was also easier to store and manipulate as a fuel. Oil-powered steamships were fast, and so crossing the Atlantic from Cherbourg to Quebec took the *Empress* a mere four-and-a-half days. During this time, Jeffrey and his fellow passengers found their sea legs and overcame their seasickness.

There had to be a wide range of facilities on board to keep the passengers amused for such a long time afloat, and allow them to feel at home. The first few days provided ample opportunity for Mr and Mrs Jeffrey to explore their ship:

'Up and down the promenade decks to the Winter Garden with its tropical plants, the lounge with its acres of comfortable chairs, the palm garden, the smoking room – a double-decker, with its fine mural oil paintings – the ballroom with its polished floor which on Sundays became a chapel, the dining saloon full of flowers, and the gymnasium with its bicycles, its mechanical horse, its rowing machines and punch balls and the various forms of apparatus which help, with the aid of the instructor, to keep sedentary passengers fit.'

It was also vital to organise meal arrangements with the senior steward as soon as possible. Passengers were allocated their evening meal times and tables at the onset of the voyage, and they had to keep to them throughout their time on board. So if you didn't want an early meal in a remote corner of the saloon for the whole voyage you had to get to the steward quickly before all the prime times and locations were taken. Meals were announced by a bugler who played a different tune for each of the main meals of the day – breakfast, lunch, and dinner – and the range of fare on offer was staggering. In 1931, Marion Bridie counted 115 separate items on the lunch menu alone.

Although the ship could stock up on food at its various ports of call, the *Empress* carried an enormous larder on sailing from Southampton. This included 75,000 pounds of beef, 3,830 chickens, 6,000 pounds of tea, 23,000 pounds of butter, 115,000 pounds of potatoes, 200,000 oranges, 1,000 gallons of milk, 4,500 bottles of spirits and 100 tons of ice.

Jeffrey and his wife soon learned that their vessel had all the amenities of a modern hotel of the period: it even had a lift. Their room was handsomely furnished and had a regular bed, not a bunk; it had a private bath and toilet, as did many on the ship, and its own electric fan. A Canadian Pacific advert of the time described the passenger services on board: 'Stenographer, barber, ladies' hairdresser, masseuse, manicurist, laundry, valet service, photographer, novelty shop, wireless, daily newspaper etc'.

After crossing the Atlantic, the *Empress* steamed up the St Lawrence river and docked in Quebec, giving Jeffrey and his wife the chance to explore the old city at their leisure. On 24 November there was also the opportunity to spend two days enjoying the pleasures of New York. During these extended city stops, passengers could choose to stay on board their ship or in a hotel if they preferred.

From New York, the *Empress* headed for Madeira with around 400 passengers on board. With each day travelled southwards, the climate became warmer, and Jeffrey and the other passengers began to abandon the thick clothing they'd needed for late autumn in North America.

The fare paid by Mr and Mrs Jeffrey included most facilities on board, except for alcoholic drinks and laundry. It also included conveyance from ship to land whenever the *Empress* reached a port, and most excursions ashore. In her account, Marion Bridie commented that the only expense she had on board was laundry, haircuts and photography. Cameras were very popular in the 1930s and film could be purchased on board, and developed while still on the ship.

## Europe and the Mediterranean

At Madeira, on 9 December, the passengers celebrated the beginning of their world cruise with a ball at the Casino in Funchal. The time of the year brought an Atlantic swell which made disembarking at Madeira difficult: the ship had to anchor some distance from shore and passengers were sped landwards by motorboats.

The next day, there was an excursion up the mountain by railway to admire the view from the top, with an exhilarating return downhill on toboggan-like sledges which speedily navigated the cobbled hilly streets back to the town. After lunch the passengers returned to their ship.

At Gibraltar, two days later, the ship refuelled and the *Empress* was invaded by vendors of local goods. Jeffrey somewhat sniffily observed that excited passengers, less well-travelled than him, were 'cheerfully paying ten dollars each for shawls and scarves that can be bought anywhere in Gibraltar for two-fifty'. On disembarking, passengers took a scenic excursion by car to Europa Point.

The passengers were provided with a tour brochure outlining the all-inclusive excursions they could take whenever their ship docked. So when the *Empress* arrived at Algiers at noon the next day, Mr and Mrs Jeffrey knew what their visit to this intriguing destination would entail:

'Motor cars will be provided for visiting various places of interest, including the modern French section of the city, Jardin d'Essai, Mustapha Supérieur, Ravine du Femme Sauvage, Arab Quarter; descent from this point on foot, rejoining motor cars. Lunch will be served at the principal hotels. The evening will be free for independent action to visit the numerous cafés, theatres etc.'

Jeffrey insists that the view of the white city of Algiers from the sea was one of the most beautiful sights in the world, so echoing the view of Thomas Dallam 327 years earlier (Chapter 1). The ship docked at an immense pontoon which enabled the passengers to reach the shore, where 150 motor cars awaited them. After their city tour and lunch, they returned to the ship and departed for Italy.

A long line of cars awaited them again at Monte Carlo where the bright sunshine revealed beautiful views during their scenic drive. They had lunch, and later visited the gaming tables which Jeffrey describes – contrary to expectation – as rather disappointingly unlike the playground of the rich.

They returned to the ship for a picturesque cruise along the Ligurian coastline – often then known simply as the 'Riviera' – and Jeffrey was able to admire the entrancing views of white villas and dark olive woods. When they awoke the next morning, the *Empress* was anchored in the Bay of Naples. It was 18 December and the sun was bright, the sky blue, and smoking Mount Vesuvius towered impressively in the background.

Jeffrey noted the huge improvements to the unappealing city of Naples thanks to the 'wise autocracy of Mussolini', and he and the other passengers took their eagerly-anticipated excursion to Pompeii, and Vesuvius obligingly erupted for them.

## The Middle East

The *Empress* reached Haifa in modern Israel on Christmas Eve, where a special train had been laid on to take passengers to Jerusalem. On arrival some went to tour Bethlehem before attending midnight mass, while others joined in carol singing in Jerusalem. After two days celebrating Christmas and sightseeing, they all boarded a luxurious sleeper train for the long trip to Cairo.

Upon arrival on 28 December, they were reunited with their luggage which had been brought down to their hotel from the *Empress* which had traversed the Suez Canal and lay at anchor at the port of Suez.

The 1920s were an exciting time to be in Cairo. Howard Carter had uncovered the tomb of Tutankhamen in 1922 – only four years before Mr and Mrs Jeffrey arrived – and the treasures of the young pharaoh had recently been put on public display in the Cairo Museum. It is impossible to overstate the enormous media and public interest in Egyptology at this time, and so this arm of the world cruise had been very keenly awaited. As a result, Canadian Pacific had devoted four complete days to sightseeing – museums, bazaars, the pyramids, mosques, temples, tombs, the desert, the Nile and the Sphinx – plus an additional full day to celebrate the New Year.

## Games on Board

The passengers left Cairo by train bound for Suez, where they once more boarded the *Empress of Scotland*. Now began a long run of uninterrupted sea travel as the ship headed through the Red Sea and the Indian Ocean. Unlike Herbert Watts, nearly 40 years before (Chapter 12), Jeffrey and his fellow passengers were spared the overbearing heat that is common in this part of the world.

It took eight days to reach their next destination of Bombay, and during this time the passengers had to keep themselves amused. Apart from those already alluded to, the *Empress* had a variety of other facilities on board to entertain its passengers during their long time at sea. These included an extensive library packed with books on travel and foreign countries; card rooms where whist and bridge were played but also other games such as chess, and particularly mah-jong which was enormously popular in the 1920s. There were tennis courts on the boat deck which were always heavily used, and even a golf practice machine. On the lower deck an open-air swimming pool was filled with seawater to help passengers cool off during the hottest parts of the cruise.

However, passengers have always enjoyed playing games on deck to pass the time. These included deck quoits, with passengers trying to throw their rings onto pegs, into buckets, or to land on squares marked out on the deck.

Shuffleboard was another popular entertainment, where pucks were pushed with a wooden paddle to glide into marked scoring areas on the deck.

During the course of a long voyage various competitions might be organised, often by a passenger-led entertainments committee assisted by the stewards. Events that might be staged included obstacle courses, cork-and-spoon races, chess tournaments, tugs-of-war, sack races, tennis matches and chalking the pig's eye (similar to pinning the tail on the donkey). A social directress and staff captain would help passengers arrange their own parties, meetings or even concerts if they wished.

Yet of all the on-board entertainments, the fancy dress parties were one of the most popular. Jeffrey does not mention them in his account, but their popularity was such that they would certainly have taken place. Marion Bridie mentions several – often with a different theme: children, books, or Japanese, for example. Passengers might be given a free choice of costume, but sometimes chief stewards would insist that passenger costumes be decided by drawing lots, with the person concerned then having to improvise with whatever he or she could find in the time available.

Every day there were performances by the ship's musicians to accompany meals but also as impromptu means of entertainment during the day; the *Empress* had both an orchestra and a jazz band. Food was a cornerstone of the passenger experience during a world cruise and the evening meal, particularly, was a special occasion enhanced by it being customary to dress for the event. While the musicians played, passengers selected their courses from a menu that resembled that of a first-class hotel of the period. Dances were also organised in the evenings after passengers had finished eating. Generally the ship's officers ordered 'lights out' at 11 o'clock in the evening, unless there was a late night event, although an extra hour of illumination was allowed in the smoke room.

## India and South East Asia

On 10 January, the *Empress* docked at Bombay (modern Mumbai), and her passengers began a seven-day sightseeing tour of the city, plus a trip by train to Agra to visit the Taj Mahal and the fascinating city of Fatehpur Sikri. Jeffrey and his wife viewed the many impressive buildings and teeming streets of

Bombay, the Caves of Elephanta and, with a certain morbid fascination, the burning ghats and Towers of Silence – both used for disposing of the dead.

In between stops, passengers zealously wrote letters and postcards to send back home, knowing that they could post them at the next port. Letters sent to passengers on the ship were collected whenever the ship docked, prompting an eager queue at the ship's postal collection point of those keen to learn news of kindred back home. After all, it was a long time to be away – and in many cases the longest time that any of the passengers had ever been absent from home. News concerning the ship itself – daily activities, weather reports etc – were conveyed to passengers by a daily ship's newspaper, which carried major media stories from Europe and America as well.

A three-day trip by sea brought the *Empress of Scotland* to Colombo, the capital of Ceylon (modern Sri Lanka) on 20 January. Here, four days were devoted to sightseeing and Jeffrey describes a beautiful drive by car that took him and his wife to the ancient and beautiful capital of Kandy, where he visited the Temple of the Tooth, tea and rubber plantations, botanical gardens, and watched elephants.

Once back on board their ship, the next highlight of the cruise came at sea. On 26 January, the *Empress* arrived at the Equator off the coast of Sumatra. One of the crew members dressed up as King Neptune and invited passengers to participate in a crossing the line ceremony, echoing the experiences of Shaw, Graham and Davies in other chapters. The passengers who wished to participate were shaved then dunked in seawater, before receiving their certificates denoting Neptune's 'freedom of the sea'.

After a day exploring Sumatra, the *Empress* set sail for Java, arriving on 30 January. She then cruised onwards to Singapore – at the time the fifth largest seaport in the world. By 7 February their ship had passed through great shoals of flying fish to reach Manila, the capital of the 7,000 or so islands that comprise the Philippines. Here, the ship was welcomed by a brass band and flowers, and a special dance was held for the passengers at the Santa Ana Cabaret.

## China and Japan

A presentation was delivered to passengers the evening before arrival at each port, by an official cruise lecturer familiar with the history and customs of each country visited. Passengers were shown slides of notable places to visit, and given notes to take away with them so that they were fully prepared in order to get the most from their visit. The lecturer would also give tips on the best items to buy when shopping.

When the *Empress of Scotland* docked at Hong Kong, the city was then part of the British Empire. However, the ship's arrival marked the beginning of nearly three weeks' sightseeing in the vicinity of China, as the cruise itinerary describes:

### HONG KONG

- There is a frequent ferry service between Kowloon and Hong Kong, and tickets will be provided for members of the cruise.
- On the first evening, passengers will be conveyed to the famous Repulse Bay Hotel, where a Chinese dinner will be given, followed by a dance.
- Motor trip will be made around the island, calling at Aberdeen and Repulse Bay, returning via Causeway Bay.
- Visits will be made to Victoria Peak, the foreign residential section, by motor-cars or trams. Sedan chairs, carried by two coolies, will be provided at the top of the peak.

### SHANGHAI

Motor trip will be made to all points of interest, including the Bund, French Bund, Chinese Bund, Lungwha Pagoda, Nanyang College, Fuh Tan University, St John's University, foreign residential section, Bubbling Well Road, Racecourse etc. Lunch will be provided on shore.

### PEKING

All members of the cruise will be given three days in Peking, with meals and lodging at the principal hotels. There will be a comprehensive programme of sightseeing, including visits to the Chinese City, Tartar City, Temple of Heaven, Confucian Temple, Hall of Classics, Summer Palace, and a special trip to the Great Wall of China.

Yet although Jeffrey and his wife enjoyed Hong Kong, the sightseeing didn't go entirely to plan in Shanghai. In the build-up to the Chinese Civil War, many of the tourist sights were in the hands of the military and therefore closed, and the roads were often blocked by barbed-wire barricades and machine gun posts. There were soldiers everywhere, and the hotels were full of refugees.

Arriving at Chin Wang Tao (modern Qinhuangdao) on 20 February, the *Empress* disgorged her passengers who took a special train to Peking (now known as Beijing). Jeffrey praises Canadian Pacific's diligence in getting this under way speedily and was impressed by the high standards achieved on the train: it was steam-heated, had four dining cars with 'wonderful' meals, and each passenger was given an illustrated guide showing points of interest along the way. Despite soldiers slowing their journey somewhat, Jeffrey's party did manage to see all the sights they expected to, and towards the end of February were once more back on board the *Empress*.

On 28 February, the *Empress of Scotland* dropped anchor at Kobe, Japan. Jeffrey was depressed that the country seemed ruined by ugly industrialisation and modern buildings quickly erected to replace those lost in recent earthquakes. However, the party moved on to Kyoto, Yokohama, Tokyo and Nikko. Jeffrey relished his tours of temples, markets, and factories, and their visit to the theatre.

## Homeward Bound

As the *Empress* steamed away from Japan, the passengers knew they were now on the last leg of their world cruise, bound towards North America. Their ship stopped at Hawaii on 12 March, where they were greeted with traditional flower garlands at Honolulu, before moving on to Hilo. At both stops, cars were put at their disposal for scenic drives around each island and the party had their second encounter of the cruise with an active volcano.

By 23 March, the ship had reached San Francisco for a two-day stopover, and this was followed by a nine-day Pacific cruise down the west coast of America to the Panama Canal. Here, the *Empress* ascended via two locks into Miraflores Lake, and then via a third lock to Gatun Lake, before descending back to sea level on the Atlantic side via a series of three further locks. The entire journey through the canal took eight hours, and Canadian Pacific was charged £5,000 for the privilege.

Steaming ever onwards, the *Empress* stopped first at Havana in Cuba for two days and then in New York for five days, before finally leaving for Europe on Good Friday, 5 April 1927. A great many of the passengers had now departed, having returned to their home in the USA or Canada. The remaining passengers staged the traditional concert in the mid-Atlantic to raise funds for seamen's charities, as Phoebe Amory witnessed on *Lusitania* in 1915. Jeffrey himself was chairman of the concert organising committee.

During the rest of the voyage home, Jeffrey and his wife asked the crew if they could explore parts of the ship that they had not previously had time to investigate, such as the engine rooms and the bakeries. This view into life 'behind the scenes' gave the Jeffreys a greater insight into the miracle that had been their round the world cruise. Their voyage had involved travelling around 36,000 miles and lasted 158 days, during which time they had received extraordinary care, courtesy and attention. It had been a real triumph of organisation and Canadian Pacific prided itself that it organised everything 'in-house', and did not farm it out to other companies.

*Chapter Sixteen*

# Honeymooners in the Great Depression

## *(1930, Mr and Mrs Hunt,* Pieter Corneliszoon Hooft*)*

James Henry Hunt had just married. At 33 years of age, he had begun to think he might never tie the knot, but then he met Jane Moore. He wanted to take his new wife on a honeymoon cruise, but unfortunately they had little money. James was an accountant for a small business in Cheshire and the amount of leave he could take was also limited. However, he was determined to travel in luxury to celebrate their marriage, but how could he make his money go as far as possible?

### Travel on a Budget

All the voyages described so far in this book have involved British ships. There is a simple reason for this – by the nineteenth century Britain was the largest ship-owning nation in the world. In 1900, the British Empire owned over 40% of all ships afloat, a dominance that was to continue until after the Second World War. Yet there were foreign companies that operated from British ports too, and they could sometimes offer more economic rates to people with a restricted budget. Many foreign ships couldn't compete with the large British companies such as Cunard, White Star, and P&O in terms of luxury, speed of travel or reputation but they could be more affordable.

Having said this, the Depression of 1929 had drastically affected world trade, with the result that most shipping companies had borne heavy losses. Many of them were forced to take vessels out of service, or even scrap some, to reduce their costs, and it was made all the worse by the fact that transport prices were generally quoted in sterling, and the pound had had to be devalued. For passengers, however, it did mean that shipping companies were desperate for business and this kept prices competitive and low. Yet what should James do? Maybe go somewhere second class but with a prestigious company like P&O? Or could he still afford to travel first class with a less well-known shipping line?

James went to an agent for advice. In the nineteenth century, passengers often booked with the shipping company directly, but by the twentieth century the large number of potential carriers, and the complex array of routes, classes of travel and destinations had encouraged the growth of businesses that could handle all your travel arrangements for you. James visited the 'passenger agent' D.H. Drakeford for advice, and he soon settled on a short trip to Genoa in Italy with the Dutch company Nederland Royal Mail Line (known as *Stoomvaart Maatschappij Nederland* or 'SMN' in the rest of Europe).

Their ship was the *Pieter Corneliszoon Hooft* bound from Southampton to Java in Indonesia, but by travelling only as far as the Mediterranean, he and his wife could still afford to travel first class, allowing James to give Jane the luxury he wanted her to have at the beginning of their new life together. It also meant he wouldn't have to ask for too much time off work. To make the trip more affordable, James decided to take the ship to Genoa but return home overland by train. The total cost of their voyage would be £34 for both him and his wife, to include all meals on board.

The Nederland Royal Mail Line was badly hit by the Depression and in 1930, had to take 16 ships out of service. Its most prestigious and lucrative run was to what was then called the Dutch East Indies, but now called Indonesia, and in particular to Batavia, the capital of the island of Java (modern Jakarta). Times were so hard that the frequency of sailing to this destination had to be cut from once a week to once every three weeks, and it was on this route that James and Jane Hunt were to travel part-way.

## Their Ship

The honeymooners' vessel, *Pieter Corneliszoon Hooft* or '*PC Hooft*', was named after a seventeenth century Dutch writer and historian. Built in France, she was launched in 1925 and was not a large ship, having a gross tonnage of 14,642, and was a little over 500 feet long. The owners intended to appeal mainly to the upper end of the travel market, by incorporating berths for 284 first class passengers, 238 second class, yet only 58 third class.

In the industry, *PC Hooft* acquired the reputation of being an 'unlucky' ship because she caught fire twice while she was being fitted out with passenger accommodation and facilities. Eventually she made her maiden voyage in 1926, so was only four years old when the Hunts sailed in her. However, she was a slow ship for the period and could only make around 16 knots when the fastest liners at this time were making speeds of over 27 knots. To put this in perspective, *PC Hooft*'s top speed had been routinely attained by P&O's Jubilee fleet in the 1880s. A few weeks after the Hunts sailed in her, the ship was taken out of service so that more powerful engines could be fitted.

The Hunts boarded their ship at Southampton on 5 June 1930. *PC Hooft* was a slim ship with a black hull, white upper decks and a single yellow funnel with a black cap. Their cabin was small but the standard size for first class on the ship – about six feet by twelve – and was pleasantly furnished with two beds, a wardrobe, a folding chair and a patterned carpet. There was an electric light, a large porthole and two washbasins, although passengers' baths and toilets were in a series of rooms opposite their cabin.

*PC Hooft* had six decks accessible to passengers, stacked one above the other and referred to by the letters A to F. The Hunts' room was well forward on the third of these, on 'C' deck, which meant they had a commanding view from their room across the ocean. Immediately above them was the large first class promenade deck, music room and library, with the first class dining room two decks below, on 'E' deck.

The hustle and bustle of a ship making ready to sail did not interrupt their enjoyment of exploring their temporary home. Their pilot came on board to navigate them down the Solent. Two tugs attached themselves to the ship – one to the stern and one to the bows – and with the mooring hawsers cast off, they swung the *PC Hooft* seawards and towed her clear of the land. Once the tugs had disengaged they were soon racing down the Solent.

## Enjoying the Facilities

The honeymoon voyage was to last just seven days but with everything laid on for them on board, they would take pleasure in every moment. One of the first pleasures was simply watching the shore speed by. Nederland Line provided passengers with a travel guide in English, containing maps and a commentary, so that they knew what to look out for. Historic Portsmouth soon approached with its naval base, then the Isle of Wight with the Needles lighthouse, where the ship slackened speed to drop off the pilot. The English Channel is a busy waterway, and there were always plenty of other ships in sight. From the Needles it was full speed ahead on a south-westerly course.

The Hunts retired to their cabin after their first evening meal, and when they arose next morning they were already off Ushant, the north-westerly point of France. From here *PC Hooft* entered the Bay of Biscay where the honeymoon couple first began to feel the heave of the Atlantic.

However, they were lucky with the weather throughout their cruise, and James and Jane enjoyed calm seas and pleasant afternoons resting in their deckchairs in the sunshine. From their usual seats they could hear the band giving its afternoon concert each day.

It became hotter as they ventured further south but both were prepared for this – Jane with her three-quarter length dresses and floppy sunhat, and James with his white open-neck shirt, sports jacket, Panama hat and habitual cigarette. They regularly walked the decks on a 'constitutional' and, probably with an eye on their post-marital plans, took particular delight in watching the children playing in the area that was specially set apart for them, high up on 'A' deck.

They also took full advantage of the never-ending supplies of drinks offered to them while they relaxed and the phrase 'my wife always has five cups of tea' became something of a holiday catchphrase. Their deck steward was particularly attentive, which they very much appreciated. However, he was a native of Indonesia, and in a disappointing reflection of the era, the Hunts did not attempt to learn his real name but simply called him 'Ooloo Booloo'.

Generally, the facilities on board were of good quality but were limited compared to a more up-market, larger, ship: there was no swimming pool, for example, and no gym or cinema. However, the Hunts both enjoyed playing tennis on the courts on 'B' deck, as well as the other traditional deck pursuits such as quoits and shuffleboard. The ship's decor was simple in the cabins, but showed a similar exuberance of style to other ships of the era in large communal areas such as the music saloon. The Hunts had been given a camera as a wedding present so they kept a photographic record of their time on the ship.

The shore receded from the Hunts' view once past Ushant, until they approached Cape Finisterre in northwest Spain. From here they hugged the shoreline of Spain and then Portugal – sometimes less than a mile offshore – until they reached the Straits of Gibraltar. Despite being the entrance to the Mediterranean, this is a comparatively narrow waterway at only three miles, but it was a very busy one. *PC Hooft* sped past the impressive rock, white houses, and guns of Gibraltar and headed through the deep blue water towards the North African coast where she gradually came closer and closer to the shore. The Hunts could soon see vineyards, fields, mountains and pretty inshore fishing boats.

## Excursion

The ship headed for Cape Caxine, which effectively hides most of the city of Algiers until it is rounded, but once past the headland the ancient capital suddenly leapt into view. *PC Hooft* slackened speed at this point to allow a pilot to board from a steam launch, and then proceeded dead slow into the cramped harbour. The leisurely speed allowed the Hunts and the other passengers to enjoy the beauty of the Algerian capital from the sea, and James took several photographs of the mass of white buildings packed against the beautiful blue of sea and sky. Careful manoeuvring was required to swing the ship to her mooring stern first, so that her exit would be easier.

As Mr and Mrs Jeffrey appreciated on their world cruise, among the highlights of a holiday voyage in the twentieth century were the many excursions that the shipping company could arrange for its passengers whenever the vessel docked. In the twentieth century these were more organised than the largely *ad hoc* shore trips that, say, Herbert Watts experienced in the 1880s (Chapter 12). Instead of simply stepping ashore to look around for yourself, the Hunts could participate in a pre-arranged guided tour by arrangement with the purser.

The *PC Hooft* was at Algiers for only six hours, so as soon as the ship was moored to the quayside, Mr and Mrs Hunt were eager to get ashore. The couple watched as a number of wooden pontoons were tied together alongside the vessel and almost as quickly as they were brought together, a mass of small traders gathered on them. The passengers could now descend the steps fastened to the ship's side, and use the newly-assembled floating walkway to reach the quay. A blackboard at the top of the steps told them what time they had to be back on board – but first they had to navigate the local vendors on the pontoon, selling everything from baskets to musical instruments, and from ceramics to textiles. Mrs Hunt was fascinated by everything they had to offer.

James had arranged for them to take a guided excursion by car first, and they enjoyed all the principal sights of the city, as well as a wonderful view of it from the top of the overlooking hills. They then followed this up with a walking tour which was thoughtfully outlined in their Nederland Line guidebook. It was their first time on foreign soil and the exotic smells, heat, sights and sounds enthralled them. Yet all too soon it was time to get back on board.

*PC Hooft* made its way cautiously through the confined space of Algiers harbour and headed northwards. When ashore they had delighted in dining at a local restaurant, but their meals on the ship were also enjoyable. Nederland Line food was of good quality but being a small ship, the choice for each meal was not as extensive as that provided by the bigger shipping companies. They ate in the first class dining saloon which required them to sit on large tables with other passengers – each table holding six to ten people.

Their ship soon reached the Balearic Islands where the Hunts could see the beautiful Majorcan capital, Palma, with its impressive medieval cathedral. As they moved on, they saw a school of dolphins, much to Jane's delight.

The ship then swung north-east to traverse the pretty French coast at the Côte d'Azur, passing Cannes, Nice and Villefranche, before approaching their final destination of Genoa, Italy. James had booked a room for them at the Bristol and Palace Hotel, but they were sorry to leave their seven-day home where they had been able to relax all day and be waited upon by others – something that neither of them were used to. James took one last photo of Jane, and they enjoyed a final constitutional together before disembarking.

## Chapter Seventeen

# Taking an African Holiday

## *(1937, Jean Davies, MV* Boschfontein*)*

Jean Davies, an actress from Surrey, was 26 years old when she decided to accompany her Uncle Bill and Auntie Flo on a holiday to Durban, South Africa. She packed up her possessions for both holiday and voyage, and attached the orange luggage labels printed with the name of her ship that she had been sent by the shipping company. On Sunday, 12 September 1937, her parents drove her to the shipping terminal at Dover in good time and they waited for what seemed an age while their tickets were checked and they were issued with embarkation cards.

> 'At last, about two hours late, we got on to the tender which was to bring us to the ship. It was a bit rough but at the last minute Mother decided to risk it and come too – bless her! Everybody's luggage was packed on and several cars too, so with all the passengers and their friends there was a bit of a crush. We left the wharf and pulled out into the harbour and then we saw her: the ship that is to be our home for the next three weeks.'

Miss Davies' vessel was the *Boschfontein*. It was not a luxury liner. Nine years old, *Boschfontein* was primarily a cargo ship but it also held accommodation for about 50 passengers. Those travelling to South Africa might choose a four-funnel liner run by the Union Castle Line if they could afford it, since the luxury facilities on board were similar to those on the great Atlantic liners run by companies such as Cunard. The *Boschfontein*, however, was comparatively small at 427 feet long, and much more basic, but was accordingly a great deal cheaper for those travelling on a budget like the Davies family. The ship's hold carried a varied cargo, but on this occasion included a large consignment of iron girders.

*Boschfontein* boasted a smoking room, dining saloon, lounge, veranda, bathrooms and a laundry. The cabins were plainly decorated and all included properly sprung beds, not bunks. Miss Davies stayed in cabin number 49, which was pleasantly painted in brown and buff, with two wardrobes and a washbasin, but it was not *en suite*. She shared her room with Ivy Morrison, eight years her senior, a secretary from Rhodesia whom she did not meet until the voyage began.

The luggage and cars on the tender were scooped up effortlessly in large nets and swung on board by the ship's derricks. While this was going on, her auntie introduced Miss Davies to old friends of hers, the Francis family, and particularly their four-year-old daughter, Gillian, to whom Miss Davies became very attached. At 6 pm a gong was sounded and all the well-wishers had to leave. Miss Davies said her goodbyes, then rushed up on deck to wave off her mother who was now departing shorewards on the tug: 'We blew our hooters and the tug blew hers, and then they moved away. We heaved anchor and moved off almost at once. We waved for as long as we could see them and all the time we were slipping quietly out of the harbour'.

Miss Davies went down to her room to unpack, met her roommate, who made no significant impression, and then headed off for dinner. The *Boschfontein*'s small dining saloon had windows on three sides and so was bright and airy. She sat with her uncle and auntie on a long table in the middle of the saloon headed by the ship's chief engineer. Senior officers were expected to socialise with their passengers at dinner, and were allocated specific tables to assist their integration. On the first night, passengers did not need to dress for dinner and could attire themselves casually, but smart dress was expected on subsequent evenings. The passengers chose from a 'colossal menu' and Miss Davies enjoyed her meal. The diners chatted for a while but soon it was time for an early night: 'The ship is as steady as a rock and except for a slight vibration, you would never know you were at sea. My bed is very comfy and there is a light over the head and a hook to hang your watch on'.

## Life on Board

The next day, Miss Davies was woken at 7 am by a knock on the door from a steward who had brought her a glass of orange juice. She decided to take a bath and walked down the corridor to a washroom but the ship was rolling quite a lot and she 'felt extremely odd when I saw the water standing at extraordinary angles in the bath'. A pre-breakfast bath was to become a daily habit.

Breakfast was at 8.30, and after that she sat on deck with her uncle and auntie, but had to wrap up in blankets because it was cold. She read for a while and then walked the decks to explore the ship. The ship was still rolling as they sailed past the French coast. Leaning over the side to watch the sea, however, was fatal! She started to feel seasick, and soon had to race back to the side of the ship to jettison her breakfast; retiring to her cabin, she sipped beef tea and gradually felt better – especially when lying down. She managed a few games of ping-pong (table tennis) with her uncle during the afternoon but couldn't face dinner and sat in her cabin nibbling rusks instead.

Tuesday morning was better and Miss Davies was able to eat breakfast as the Spanish shoreline raced by. 'The rollers seemed enormous and we saw a small fishing boat with a very strange rig that kept getting completely out of sight in the troughs of the waves'. She also saw a whale blowing close to the ship that was 'most thrilling'.

As she watched, Miss Davies spoke to a sailor who was keeping a lookout for mines. 'Unpleasant thought!' she wrote. The mines had been laid by Nationalists in the Spanish Civil War and are a reminder that in less than two years Europe would be embroiled in the Second World War. Passenger ships would again become victims of mines and U-boats as the *Lusitania* had in the previous conflict: the first British ship destroyed would be the SS *Athenia* on 3 September 1939, with over 1,400 people on board (although all but 117 survived).

Meanwhile, Miss Davies's most immediate concerns on the *Boschfontein* were far less serious. She simply sought to keep herself amused. Entertainment on board was quite limited: there was no orchestra, gym, library, shops, organised shore excursions, lectures, cinema or casino. Just various deck games, socialising with the other people on board, and the books that passengers had brought with them. It was very different to the experiences of passengers on twentieth century luxury liners such as the *Lusitania* or *Empress*, as described in earlier chapters. Her uncle headed the passengers' committee to organise entertainments such as tennis tournaments and the fancy dress party.

Fortunately, Miss Davies was very sociable and quickly made new friends. She enjoyed after-dinner conversation, and during the course of the voyage played a lot of deck tennis. She seems to have played ping-pong every day too, and with almost everyone on board, even though she admits to being not very good at it, and in fact almost invariably lost throughout the voyage. Nonetheless, her days on the *Boschfontein* were very relaxing.

> 'Life on board is very pleasant. The feeling that there is nothing that must be done is so refreshing. Every afternoon between two and four we have to sit quiet because games etc. are not allowed, because of the people who want to sleep. Perhaps it is just as well, otherwise one would never stop: there is always someone wanting a game.'

On Wednesday there was a dance, using records to broadcast the music which was 'simply appalling'. She had a very long dance with Johnny Hofmeyr. Miss Davies spent a lot of time in Johnny's company on the voyage – a young man about her age whom she clearly found attractive – but she quickly learned that he was newly married and travelling to join his wife in Cape Town. One evening they talked alone together on deck for ages and she describes the setting romantically: 'It was gloriously warm, and the sea was a velvety midnight blue, with the tips of the waves catching the lovely silvery moonlight'.

By Thursday it was warm enough for the crew to erect the ship's temporary swimming pool and pump it full of seawater to help the passengers cool off:

> 'It is a canvas lining to the top section of one of the holds. It is about ten feet square and there is about six feet of water. It is most welcome and lovely to fall into when you are frightfully hot after playing games. It is a bit small, but adequate, and deep enough to dive for pennies in.'

The *Boschfontein* had a telegraph facility and she sent a telegram home to her parents to let them know that she was 'getting on all right'. She also wrote lots of letters to friends in England because on arrival at Dakar, in Senegal, she would be able to post them.

Evacuation procedures or 'boat drill' had to be rehearsed once during every voyage and *Boschfontein* was no exception. The chaos or confusion on some earlier shipwrecks had demonstrated the importance of both crews and passengers being prepared. The drill showed passengers what they would have to do in an emergency, and familiarised them with escape routes and the location of lifebelts. It also gave crews the opportunity to check the integrity of lifeboats and to practise launching methods.

The *Boschfontein* sailed onwards, and as they neared their destination it became hotter. Miss Davies saw wildlife she had never seen before – 'an enormous school of porpoises', 'small birds like swallows flying around the stern' and, of course, 'flocks' of flying fish. The change in climate stimulated the ship's officers to swap their thick dark blue uniforms for a cooler, white tropical version. The hot weather also, understandably, discouraged Miss Davies's interest in deck sports in the heat of the day.

## Sighting Africa

Very early on Sunday morning, Miss Davies suddenly found herself awake: 'I woke at about one o'clock and wondered what had happened. Then I realised that the engines had almost stopped. I leapt out of bed and flung on a dressing gown and rushed on deck. I got there just in time to see us glide quietly into harbour and drop anchor'.

They had arrived at Dakar, where some passengers disembarked. In the morning, she watched a lighter come alongside to refuel the ship. *Boschfontein* was a diesel-powered ship, the first vessels of this nature having been pioneered in the run-up to the First World War. Refuelling was in Miss Davies's words 'a pretty smelly but a very clean business as far as we were concerned. All they have to do is connect up a pipe to a place in the side of the ship and pump'.

Remarkably, she goes on to say: 'There were lots of niggers on the lighter, which was a terrific thrill for me, being the first I have seen. They are

Senegalese. I watched for ages'. It's shocking to realise that a well-educated woman from Britain in the late 1930s had never seen black people before. She sat and chatted to Johnny until about 3 am and then she went back to bed.

The *Boschfontein* left Dakar in the mist at about 6 am. By mid-morning, Miss Davies was once more energetically playing deck tennis and ping-pong. There was a notable first: for the only time on the voyage she beat another passenger at ping-pong – a Mr Rubens fell victim, even though he was 'usually not too bad'. And the tennis continued after tea:

'I had a frightfully energetic singles match with Johnny. He beat me 6–2, but we had lots of deuce games. I have never been quite so wet and hot in my life, but I felt grand. There is nothing like a good sweat to make you feel fit in the tropics! Rather indelicate but true!'

Sunday was a day of remarkable occurrences. It was one week into the voyage and she had seen her first black people, beaten someone at ping-pong, and to cap it all the passengers – out of the blue – started to call each other by their Christian names. For the first seven days, and totally consistent with the era, everyone had been Mr, Mrs, or Miss So-and-so. But abruptly the social barriers were down and it was all different, and Miss Davies found it liberating:

'Today has been marvellous. Everyone suddenly started calling me Jean. First Nigel Helme, then Johnny Hofmeyr, then Joyce Roskill, and then Mrs Helme. It gives you a lovely sort of a feeling when people do it without being asked. When Mr Hofmeyr had done it, he suddenly stated, without any reason: "I'm called Johnny." When I asked why he had suddenly said that, he said: "It's easier than shouting, Oi!".'

On Monday she continued to spend a lot of time with Johnny, and enjoyed a moment reminiscent of the famous scene between Leonardo DiCaprio and Kate Winslet in the film *Titanic*:

'I went up to the bows again this morning with Johnny. It is grand up there: quite the best spot in the ship. We hung right over the side and watched the bow lifting right out of the water and then coming down and cutting right through the next wave. It was simply glorious.'

After dinner that evening, Miss Davies was forced into a game she didn't want to play: 'I had to play Lexicon with the Bowens and the Edwards because I couldn't think of a sufficiently plausible excuse not to. As I had expected, Mr Bowen became slightly vulgar and not in the least funny'. Fortunately, Johnny came to her rescue and whisked her away to the secluded, moonlit bows to watch the phosphorescence on the dark ocean.

## Making Entertainment

The *Boschfontein* crossed the equator on Tuesday, 21 September. Father Neptune and his court came aboard and asked to interview all those who had never crossed the line before. Miss Davies hid and Neptune sent out pirates to find her, eventually chasing her around the decks. Perhaps predictably, Johnny was one of the pirates who found her and hauled her back to the King's presence.

'Then, after a slight argument with His Royal Highness and his wife, they decided to waste no more time and flung me firmly and bodily into the pool fully-clothed. The Purser and Mr McWilliam were dressed as negroes and stationed in the pool to see that everyone got their three duckings. They certainly made no mistake about mine! I seemed to have fooled most people into thinking that I was really scared.'

The ship's company presented a certificate to every passenger who had participated in the ceremony and thus initiated into King Neptune's realm.

The next day, Miss Davies won the daily sweepstake for guessing the number of miles that the ship ran the previous day. It only amounted to eleven shillings, but it enabled her to offer to buy drinks for her friends on board. She habitually drank mainly non-alcoholic drinks, but did allow

CERTIFICATE

To all sailors wherever you may be, and to all mermaids, sea serpents, whales, sharks, dolphins, skates, eels, suckers, lobsters, crabs, pollywogs and other living things of the sea. Greeting.

Know you that on this 21st day of September in latitude 00-00-00 and longitude 15W, there appeared within the limits of Our Royal Domain the MV *Boschfontein*.

That the said vessel and officers and crew thereof have been inspected by Ourself and Our Royal Staff. And be it known by all you sailors, marines, landlubbers and others who may be honoured by her presence that:

MISS DAVIES

having been found worthy to be numbered as one of our trusty shellbacks has been gathered to Our fold and duly initiated into the solemn mysteries of the ancient order of the deep, under the name of MINNOW.

Be it further understood that by virtue of the power invested in Me, I do hereby command all My subjects to show due honour and respect to her whenever she enters Our Realm. Disobey this order under penalty of Our Royal Displeasure.

Neptune

herself the occasional gimlet – a cocktail made from gin and lime juice. The warm, clear night was particularly entrancing:

'The moon has been perfect tonight. I spent hours just looking at it from the windows outside the smoking room. They were all open but it was as warm as anything. The masts and derricks looked so solid and stately silhouetted against the moonlit sky and just rolling very slightly across the stars. Johnny came along and showed me the Southern Cross' [a constellation].

As the voyage progressed, passengers became keen to look for diversions to entertain themselves. Some organised their own parties to celebrate a birthday or wedding anniversary, or just to enjoy hosting a social event. Johnny arranged a get-together on 24 September, for example. It was getting cooler so the swimming pool was dismantled. However, the purser ran a physical fitness class on deck when requested; there was a children's sports afternoon, a tennis tournament, and one evening a treasure hunt after dinner; on another evening there was a quiz. Miss Davies enjoyed a tour of the engine room, and had long conversations with members of the crew to try and understand their roles. The purser revealed that he had to spend so much time at sea that he had seen his wife for only 13 days in the past year.

In many ways the highlight of the entertainment on board was the fancy dress party on 25 September. Miss Davies decided to go as a child – with blue hair ribbon, a nightie, teddy bear, and shoes with white bobbles. The passengers had their evening meal in fancy dress and then there was a parade followed by a vote for best costume:

'Uncle and auntie got first prize, and Mr England and Mrs McWilliam got second. Uncle went as an eighteenth century English gentleman and looked marvellous, and auntie went as Nell Gwynne in her old age! Mr England was Mephistopheles and Mrs McWilliam had a very pretty and genuine Hungarian costume.'

The dancing continued until the small hours, but the next day was the Captain's farewell dinner – a lavish meal in which the captain makes a speech to thank his passengers and the passengers return the compliment to the ship's crew. Every passenger was given free champagne for the evening and a present from the shipping line – Miss Davies received a photograph album. The meal surpassed all expectation from a small ship.

---

### FAREWELL DINNER

---

*Caviare Béluga en belle-vue*

*Cream soup Montmorency*

*Poached Rhine salmon Brillat-Savarin*

*Medallions of venison à la Rénaissance*

*Cold Westland asparagus in mayonnaise sauce*

*Braised young turkey and mushrooms*

*Compote riche*

*Ice cream bombe 'Hawaiian girl'*

*Petits fours*

*Assorted cheese*

*Fruit*

*Delicacies*

*Mocha*

---

There were speeches after the meal, and then dancing for the rest of the evening:

'We were rolling a bit so it made things a little difficult. You suddenly found yourself rushing downhill and landing in the lap of someone who was sitting out! We danced practically without stopping from 9.30 to 1.30 am. There were very few intervals, and what there were, were very short. One dance was very hectic. When the music stops everyone changes partners, and when you are just pausing to take a breather you suddenly find yourself whirled off by someone else.'

Eventually Miss Davies went to bed at about 2 am.

## Setting Foot in Africa

The morning after, all the passengers were a little the worse for wear. The after-effects of a late night with lots of champagne, no doubt, although a surprising number of them, including Johnny, seemed suddenly to have developed 'seasickness'. The next day the *Boschfontein* arrived at Cape Town and Miss Davies admired the celebrated and magnificent view. Johnny joined her on deck and pointed out all the various peaks. 'He really has been awfully nice,' she confided to her diary, but one wonders at her true feelings when she spied Johnny's wife waiting at the dockside to meet him.

Miss Davies made her farewells to Johnny and the other passengers, including her unsociable roommate Miss Morrison, but then marched ashore to explore: 'It was a terrific thrill when I put my first foot in Africa!' She went for a long drive and admired the breath-taking scenery and beautiful flowers. The next day she toured a botanical garden and a zoo, but getting back to the ship was 'rather like getting home' and she was surprised at how much she missed it. It was particularly pleasant having a cabin now to herself.

On 30 September the *Boschfontein* left Cape Town and the next day docked at Mossel Bay. The purser advised her not to go ashore on account of the weather and she was glad she didn't because the sea was so rough that passengers returning to the ship had to be hauled aboard in a rather alarming manner:

'It was too rough for the tug to come alongside so the passengers had to be slung aboard in a basket. It was the most incredible performance and I should have been scared stiff. The basket is about six feet high and takes three people. They hoisted it up with the derricks and swung it on board. The boat got into a roll when one lot were in and they nearly got tipped out!'

On 1 October, *Boschfontein* made Port Elizabeth with some difficulty due to a strong head wind, yet once there Miss Davies raced ashore to do some sightseeing. At every port the ship dropped off a few passengers as well as a proportion of its cargo, so with each stop Miss Davies was left with progressively fewer people on board that she knew. The next day fog delayed the ship's entrance to the port of East London: Miss Davies was woken by the ship sounding her foghorn during the night.

On 4 October the *Boschfontein* pulled into Durban and Miss Davies tipped her stewards before having her last breakfast. She finished her packing and, once docked, her cousin, Guy, came aboard to welcome her to South Africa. She was so pleased to see him; she had had a wonderful trip, and was 'awfully sad at leaving the ship.' That ship had carried her 8,000 miles in just over three weeks.

The last words of this book are best left to Miss Davies, who sums up what the passenger experience had become by the late 1930s: 'I think a first voyage is one to be remembered always. It has all been quite perfect. I shall always be grateful for this voyage: it was Africa I had been looking forward to – it didn't occur to me that the journey could be so exciting'.

# Bibliography

## General Sources

Charlwood, Don, *The Long Farewell: Settlers Under Sail* (Allen Lane, Australia, 1981)

Coleman, Terry, *Passage to America: A History of Emigrants from Great Britain and Ireland to America in the Mid-nineteenth Century* (Hutchinson, London, 1972)

Greenhill, Basil & Giffard, Ann *Travelling by Sea in the Nineteenth Century: Interior Design in Victorian Passenger Ships* (Adam & Charles Black, London, 1972)

*Lloyd's Register of Shipping* for all the ships mentioned in the text

Wills, Simon, *Tracing Your Merchant Navy Ancestors* (Pen & Sword, 2012)


## Chapter 1

PRIMARY SOURCE

Bent, James Theodore (editor), *Early Voyages and Travels in the Levant: 1 – The Diary of Master Thomas Dallam 1599–1600* (Hakluyt Society, London, 1893)


## Chapter 2

PRIMARY SOURCE

Bradford, William, *History of Plymouth Plantation* (first published 1669), reprinted from the Massachusetts Historical Collection, edited by Charles Deane (Privately printed, Boston, 1856)

Arber, Edward, *The Story of the Pilgrim Fathers* (Ward & Downey Ltd, London, 1897)

Brown, Alexander, *The First Republic in America* (Houghton Mifflin & Co, Boston & New York, 1898)

Caffrey, Kate, *The Mayflower* (Andre Deutsch, 1974)

Philbrick, Nathaniel, *Mayflower: A Story of Courage, Community, and War* (Viking Press, 2006)

Villiers, Alan, *Men, Ships and the Sea* (National Geographic Society, Washington, 1963)

The Mayflower Society, www.themayflowersociety.com

Plimoth Plantation heritage website, www.plimoth.org

## Chapter 3

PRIMARY SOURCE
Ovington, John, *A Voyage to Suratt in the Year 1689* (Jacob Tonson, London, 1696)
Rawlinson, H.G. (editor), *A Voyage to Surat in the Year 1689 by J Ovington* (Oxford University Press, London, 1929 [This edition has a biography of Ovington as an Introduction])

Sutton, Jean, *Lords of the East: The East India Company and its Ships* (Conway Maritime Press, London, 1981)
East India Company Ships website www.eicships.info

## Chapter 4

PRIMARY SOURCE
Fielding, Henry, *The Journal of a Voyage to Lisbon* (A. Millar, The Strand, London, 1755)

De Castro, J. Paul, Henry Fielding's Last Voyage, *The Library* (Transactions of The Bibliographical Society), 1917, s3-VIII (30): p.145–159
Dickson, Frederick S., The early editions of Fielding's 'a Voyage to Lisbon', *The Library* (Transactions of The Bibliographical Society), 1917 s3-VIII (29): p.24–35

## Chapter 5

PRIMARY SOURCE
Schaw, Janet, *Journal by a Lady of a Voyage from Scotland to the West Indies and South Carolina, with an Account of Personal Experiences During the War of Independence and of a Visit to Lisbon on Her Return; 25 Oct. 1774–Dec. 1775.* (Manuscript held by British Library, London, ref: Egerton MS 2423)

Andrews, Evangeline Walker (Editor), *Journal of a Lady of Quality* (Yale University Press, New Haven, 1921 [A transcription of the original manuscript with analysis])
Pepys, Samuel, *The Diary of Samuel Pepys* (George Bell & Sons, London 1893)

## Chapter 6

PRIMARY SOURCE
Graham, Maria, *Journal of a Voyage to Brazil and Residence there During Part of the Years 1821, 1822, 1823* (printed for Longman etc, London, 1824)

Anon [Bechervaise, John], *Thirty-six years of a seafaring life by an old quartermaster* (W. Woodward, Portsea, 1839)

Captain's log, HMS *Doris*, Apr 1821 to December 1825 (at The National Archives, Kew, England, ref: ADM 51/3147)


## Chapter 7

PRIMARY SOURCE

Moore, George, *Journal of a Voyage Across the Atlantic – with Notes on Canada and the United States; and Return to Great Britain in 1844* (Privately printed, London, 1845)


Balch, Lewis Penn Witherspoon *et al.*, *God in the Storm, a Narrative of the Rev. L.P.W. Balch, an Address by Rev. Lyman Beecher D.D., and a Sermon by the Rev. Thomas Smyth D.D., Prepared on Board the 'Great Western', After the Storm Encountered on Her Recent Voyage*, (Robert Carter & Brothers, New York, 1847)

Dickens, Charles, *American Notes for General Circulation and Pictures from Italy* (Chapman & Hall, London, 1913)

Hosken, James, *The Logs of the First Voyage Made with the Unceasing Aid of Steam Between England and America by the 'Great Western' of Bristol* (The Mirror Office, Bristol, 1838)

Smiles, Samuel, *George Moore: Merchant and Philanthropist* (George Routledge & Sons, London, 1878)


## Chapter 8

PRIMARY SOURCE

Smith, William, *An Emigrant's Narrative or a Voice from the Steerage: Being a Brief Account of the Sufferings of the Emigrants in the Ship India on her Voyage from Liverpool to New York in the Winter of 1847–8* (privately printed, New York, 1850)


Conroy, Patrick, *Robert Whyte's Famine Ship Diary 1847: The Journey of an Irish Coffin Ship* (Mercier Press, 1989)

Giffard, Ann, *Towards Quebec: Two Mid-19th Century Emigrants' Journals* (National Maritime Museum, HMSO, 1981). [Contains full text of William Fulford's journal (1848)]

Robertson, Robert, *Observations on the Jail, Hospital, or Ship Fever* (J. Murray, London, 1783)

## Chapter 9

PRIMARY SOURCE

Neville, William Latimer (edited by Caswall, Henry), *Journal of a Voyage from Plymouth to Sierra Leone with Notices of Madeira, Teneriffe, Bathurst &c* (Bell & Daldy, London, 1858)

Barrow, Alfred Henry, *Fifty Years in Western Africa: Being a Record of the Work of the West Indian Church on the Banks of the Rio Pongo* (SPCK, London, 1900)

Crew list for SS *Armenian* (National Archives, Kew, London, ref: BT 98/5137)

## Chapter 10

PRIMARY SOURCE

Munro, John, *A Brief Narrative of the Loss of the Steam-ship 'London' in the Bay of Biscay 11th January 1866* (printed at Daily Times office, Dunedin, 1866)

Correspondence and news items from *The Ballarat Star*, *The Times*, *Illustrated London News*, *Times of India*, *The Colonist*, *The Mercury* (Hobart), *The Argus* (Melbourne), *Sydney Morning Herald* etc

Moultrie, Gerard, *Wreck of the London* (S.W. Partridge, London, 1866)

## Chapter 11

PRIMARY SOURCE

Perston, Mary Eliza, *Journal of a Voyage to Wellington Commenced March 25th 1868 in the ship 'Coleroon'* (handwritten manuscript, privately owned, 1868)

Clark, Arthur H., *The Clipper Ship Era: An Epitome of Famous American and British Clipper Ships, Their Owners, Builders, Commanders, and Crews 1843–1869* (G.P. Putnam's Sons, New York & London, 1911)

Crew list and log of the *Coleroon* (official number 23553) for 1868 via Maritime History Archive, Newfoundland www.mun.ca/mha

*The Press*, *The Star*, *Lyttelton Times*, and other New Zealand newspapers for 1868 via the National Library of New Zealand's 'Papers Past' website: http://paperspast.natlib.govt.nz

## Chapter 12

PRIMARY SOURCE

Watts, Herbert J., *Personal Diary* (handwritten manuscript, privately owned, 1888–89)

Furniss, Harry *P&O Sketches in Pen and Ink* (The Studio of Design and Illustration Supply Agency, London, 1890)

Howarth, David & Howarth, Stephen, *The Story of P&O: The Peninsular and Oriental Steam Navigation Company* (Weidenfeld and Nicolson, London, 1986)

Lilley, William Osborne, *Bound for Australia on Board the Orient: A Passenger's Log* (Andrew Crombie, Hamilton, Adams & Co., London, 1885)

Lloyd, William Whitelock, *P&O Pencillings*, (published for the Peninsular and Oriental Steam Navigation Company, London, 1892)

Padfield, Peter, *Beneath the House Flag of the P&O* (Hutchinson, London, 1981)

P&O Heritage website, www.poheritage.com

Smith, T.C., *From Great Britain to Greater Britain or a Voyage to Australia* (Guardian Printing Works, Fishergate, 1888)

## Chapter 13

PRIMARY SOURCE

Whitmarsh, Hubert Phelps, The Steerage of Today: A Personal Experience (*Century Magazine*, 1898; Vol.55, issue 4, p.528–43)

Fry, Henry, *The History of North Atlantic Steam Navigation* (Sampson Low, Marston and Company, London, 1896)

## Chapter 14

PRIMARY SOURCE

Amory, Phoebe, *The Death of the Lusitania* (William Briggs, Toronto, 1917)

Ballard, Robert D. with Dunmore, Spencer, *Exploring the Lusitania* (Weidenfeld and Nicolson, London, 1995)

Golding, Harry, *The Wonder Book of Ships* (Ward, Lock & Co Ltd, London, 1922)

Hickey, Des & Smith, Gus, *Seven Days to Disaster: The Sinking of the Lusitania* (Collins, London, 1981)

Simpson, Colin, *Lusitania* (Book Club Associates, London, 1972)

Lusitania Resource website, www.rmslusitania.info

## Chapter 15

PRIMARY SOURCE

Jeffrey, Percy Shaw *Round the World with an Empress by Canadian Pacific* (Ed. J. Burrows & Co. Ltd, 1928)

Brassey, Annie, *A Voyage in the "Sunbeam" Our Home on the Ocean for Eleven Months* (Longmans Green & Co., London, 1880)

Bridie, Marion Ferguson, *Round the World Without a Pinprick* (Jones & Co, Birmingham, 1933)

Burdick, Joel W., *Our World Tour 1922–23* (originally published by Warde Press, Pittsburgh, 1923 but reprinted by National Museums & Galleries on Merseyside in 1990)

Lever, William Hesketh, *Following the Flag: Jottings of a Jaunt Round the World* (Simpkin Marshall & Co. Ltd, London, 1893)

Lord Northcliffe, *My Journey Round the World 1921–22* (John Lane, The Bodley Head Ltd, London, 1923)

## Chapter 16

PRIMARY SOURCE

Hunt, James, photograph album and scrapbook of honeymoon voyage (handwritten manuscript, privately owned, 1930)

Anon., *Travel Guide of the Nederland Royal Mail Line*, Amsterdam (undated but approx. 1925)

de Boer, G.J., *The Centenary of the Stoomvaart Maatschappij 'Nederland' 1870–1970* (World Ship Society, Kendal, 1970)

## Chapter 17

PRIMARY SOURCE

Davies, Jean, *South African Adventure. Part 1: Outward Bound on the M.V. Boschfontein* (typewritten manuscript, privately owned, 1937)

*Holland Afrika Lijn*, undated promotional brochure with fleet particulars, approx. 1934

## Now read Simon Wills' first novel …

# Lifeboatmen

*"Men died and no-one likes it. Your job was to save them.*
*That's what the lifeboat's <u>for</u>."*

A true story of shipwrecks, a hurricane, courtroom drama, and a community split down the middle. A tale from the early days of the lifeboat service, when not everything went according to plan.

Simon Wills recreates the small seafaring town of Poole, Dorset, in 1866. The arrival of a new lifeboat prompts a disparate band of men to volunteer to serve in her. But none of them are prepared for the extraordinary conditions they face on their very first call-out.

Yet their lack of success in saving lives is met not with commiseration, but condemnation. Lowly lifeboatmen are pitted against the full force of the ruling class and the media. An embattled coxswain, a critical Mayor, sailors' bodies washed ashore, and an inexperienced lifeboat crew.

Heavily criticized for failing to save lives, can the Dorset lifeboatmen learn to rescue those in distress as well as their own reputations?

## Praise for *Lifeboatmen*

'An inspiring tale of redemption.'
*Who Do You Think You Are? Magazine*

'An impressive blending of historical fact and great storytelling. An authentic and fast-paced fictional presentation of this enthralling story.'
*Discover Your History*

'The story moves along at a nail-biting pace, while the colourful descriptions capture the essence of the period in a seafaring community on the cusp of change.'

*Family Tree Magazine*

'It's a wonderful read. It's so fast-paced as well – you really get that sense of urgency.'

*Katie Martin, BBC Radio Solent*

*Lifeboatmen*, by Simon Wills (Pen & Sword, 2014, ISBN-10: 1783462884) is published by Pen & Sword (www.pen-and-sword.co.uk). Hardback edition RRP £16.99.